Garden
Projects

THE BEST OF
FINE GARDENING

Garden Projects

The Taunton Press

Cover photo: Ruth Lively

Back-cover photos: left, Rita Buchanan;
top center, Tom Roster; bottom center,
Roger Holmes; right, Chris Curless

for fellow enthusiasts

First printing: June 1994
Printed in the United States of America

A FINE GARDENING Book

FINE GARDENING® is a trademark of The Taunton Press, Inc.,
registered in the U.S. Patent and Trademark Office.

The Taunton Press
63 South Main Street
Box 5506
Newtown, CT 06470-5506

Library of Congress Cataloging-in-Publication Data

Garden projects.
        p.   cm. — (The Best of Fine gardening)
      Articles originally published in Fine gardening magazine.
      "A Fine gardening book" — T.p. verso.
      Includes index.
      ISBN 1-56158-085-6
      1. Garden structures — Design and construction.
      I. Fine gardening. II. Series.
TH4961.G373   1994   94-1480
    717 — dc20   CIP

Contents

Introduction

Here are the best of the articles on garden and landscape projects profiled by *Fine Gardening* magazine in its first five years of publication.

In this beautifully illustrated collection, expert home gardeners, horticulturists and landscape contractors outline in detail many common projects that can enhance just about any property. Among the articles included, you'll find first-hand accounts of how to build a traditional picket fence, a fish pond that's functional as well as beautiful, and a dry-stone retaining wall. Ranging from the tried-and-true to the innovative, the approaches recommended by the authors can be applied in a variety of landscape situations.

You'll find the articles in this collection especially helpful and inspiring because they are the work of enthusiasts who have actually completed these projects successfully themselves. Sharing their hard-won experience, the authors tell you how to succeed with the projects in your own yard.

The editors of *Fine Gardening* hope you'll experiment with the ideas in this collection of articles. No matter which you choose to try, your efforts will be rewarded.

"The Best of *Fine Gardening*" series collects articles from back issues of *Fine Gardening* magazine. A note on p. 96 gives the date of first publication for each article; product availability, suppliers' addresses and prices may have changed since then. This book is the sixth in the series.

Paths of Brick

How to pave your way through the garden without mortar or concrete

A broad path of bricks laid in herringbone pattern offers a distinctive entrance to a sunken garden. Enduring and beautiful, brick walks can also be easy to install.

All photos: Chris Curless

by Richard T. Kreh, Sr.

Among the many ways to get from here to there in a garden, few are as attractive, inviting and easy to traverse as a brick walkway. And you can choose from a wide range of colors, textures, shapes and brick-laying patterns to design a walk that is a unique garden feature.

You don't need special skills to build a brick walk if you lay it dry. I know—I've been a mason all my life. In a dry-laid walk, the bricks rest on layers of stone and sand (the stone dust allows water to drain through, and the sand provides a cushion for minor adjustments). There's no concrete to pour, no mortar to hold the bricks in place. Better yet, a dry-laid walk is more durable than a mortared one. When the ground freezes and thaws (a common phenomenon in all but the mildest-winter climates), it causes the soil to heave, or lift upwards. A mortared walk eventually cracks, but a dry-laid walk moves with the ground. If the walk settles unevenly, just lift a few bricks, level the ground beneath them, and set the bricks back in place.

A walk as you like it

Consider appearance and placement when you plan a brick walk. If your garden is formal, then a straight, square walk makes the most sense. In a garden where curving lines dominate or where the look is more natural, an irregular or curving walk that flows with the layout of the garden is probably more appropriate. The most direct path is often not the most appealing—a sinuous walk or one that jogs left or right on the way to its destination adds a distinctive element to a landscape.

Give some thought to the width of the walk. I consider 3 ft. a minimum width for a brick path—it allows two people to walk abreast or to pass each other comfortably. A front walk should be about 4 ft. wide, which allows for more traffic and is more inviting.

The pattern in which you lay the bricks affects the walkway's appearance. Because bricks are uniform in shape, they can be laid in a variety of patterns, or bonds. There are three basic patterns—running bond, basket weave and herringbone. (See drawings at right.) Most of the other patterns are

variations on these three. Running bond is the simplest and the most familiar pattern—the bricks in neighboring rows are staggered. It's easy to install—you have to cut bricks only at the beginning and the end of the walk.

The basket-weave pattern, which looks like its namesake, is formed by laying two bricks side by side, turning the next two 90°, and repeating the process. The change in direction is very pleasing to the eye. The basket weave requires a little more skill to install than the running bond does because bricks vary slightly in size; keeping the pattern straight requires minor shifting of bricks here and there.

Of the three basic brick-laying patterns, the herringbone pattern is by far the most intricate and difficult to install, but it locks together and resists movement better than the others. The herringbone pattern is a variation on running bond. Instead of being laid in straight rows, the bricks run at a 45°

angle to the edge and meet end-to-side (rather than end-to-end). Since all of the bricks along the edge of the walk must be cut at 45° angles, you'll have to develop brick-cutting skills.

At the planning stage, you also need to decide whether you want a border for your walkway. A border can be composed of bricks set in a position different from the pattern of the walk (end up, for example) or it can be made of a variety of other materials, such as landscaping timbers, railroad ties or stone. Many masons insist on installing a border to prevent the bricks from shifting, but I don't think one is necessary in most cases. Still, many people think a border gives a walkway a more finished appearance.

Before you choose the location for your walkway, think about what lies below ground. You don't want to slice through underground wiring or plumbing as you excavate the bed. Even

Paving patterns

Because bricks are uniform in size, you can lay them in a variety of patterns, or bonds. The three most common patterns are running bond, basket weave and herringbone. Most other patterns are variations of these three.

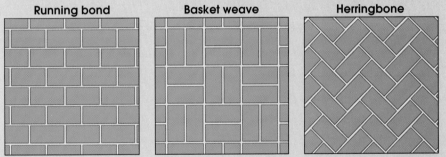

Running bond   **Basket weave**   **Herringbone**

A colorful cross section reveals the foundation of a dry-laid brick walkway. The bottom layer is blue-gray stone dust, which compacts solidly and resists settling (fine gravel also works well). A 1-in. bed of golden sand tops the stone dust.

A 2×4 screed distributes a bed of sand evenly over a layer of stone dust. The notched ends of the screed slide over the tops of the temporary wooden forms at the edges of the walk.

width) of your walk. I estimate four and a half bricks per square foot, regardless of paving pattern. If you want a brick border around the walk, you have to add some extra bricks. You also need to allow for misshapen and broken bricks. I generally add five percent as a cushion. If you end up with extra bricks, keep them on hand for small repair jobs.

For a dry-laid walkway, you'll also need sand and finely crushed gravel (also called stone dust or stone screenings). You can buy them in bulk from a sand and gravel dealer. If you can't get stone dust, buy fine gravel. (Ask for ⅝-in. chips or common pea gravel.) For most climates, 1 in. of sand and 3 in. of stone dust (or gravel) is sufficient for the bed. The sand and gravel dealer can calculate the quantities you'll need from the square footage of your walk.

A level foundation

You'll have to excavate to get the level of your finished walk at or slightly above the soil level. First make a digging guide. Lay out a short section of walk, placing the bricks on top of the ground in the pattern you intend to use. Then measure about 6 in. from either side of the bricks to determine the width of the excavation. (The extra space allows room for work space and 2×4s which serve as temporary bricklaying forms.) Pound small stakes into the ground at these two points. For straight walks, I do the same at the other end and stretch a nylon line between the stakes at each end.

If your walk is curved, determine the outlines of the excavation with garden hoses. Move the hoses around until you get the curve you want. Then mark their position by filling a small funnel with powdered, hydrated lime (available from building-supply stores) and let the lime sift out next to the hose, using your finger as a release control.

To figure how deep to dig, add together the thickness of a brick and 4 in. for the sand and stone dust. Dig out the base of the walk with standard hand tools—pick, mattock, shovel and rake. If you don't already have one, consider investing in a square-point shovel, which has a flat blade. It's ideal for removing soil and for slicing thin layers off the bottom of the excavation. Stop occasionally to check the depth. I lay a plank across the excavation and measure down with a tape or a ruler.

if the underground utilities are well below excavation depth, the day may come when they will require service and your walk will have to be torn up. The plot plan of your house may show where wires and pipes run. You should also ask your local utility companies to come out and mark the location of the lines; there's usually no charge for this service.

To save yourself time and trouble, I recommend that you put your ideas on paper. Draw different patterns, borders and walk shapes to see which you prefer. I use ¼-in. graph paper. Because the standard brick is twice as long as it is wide (8 in. × 4 in.), I let every two blocks represent one full brick. Keep in mind that your design won't work out exactly when you actually lay the bricks—bricks aren't perfect and neither are you.

Bricks that last

I recommend you buy only bricks made specifically for paving. Bricks in walks are subjected to traffic and moisture, and in most of the U.S. they must

also endure repeated freezing and thawing. Bricks that are made for house walls can quickly deteriorate under such conditions. The American Society for Testing and Materials (ASTM), an industry association that sets specifications for building materials, has described the manufacturing requirements for paving bricks in its "Standard Specification for Pedestrian and Light Traffic Paving Brick" (ASTM C 902). Ask your supplier if the bricks you want to buy conform to this specification.

Avoid used or salvaged bricks. Their rustic or historic look may make them appealing, but in my experience, most aren't durable over the long haul. If you want the look of old bricks, select new reproductions.

The best place to buy bricks is at a local masonry-supply company listed in the yellow pages of the phone book under "Brick." Specialty companies have the best prices and the widest selection. Many also have a showroom of samples.

To order bricks, you'll need to calculate the square footage (length ×

Forms ease the work

To hold the bricks (or the border) in place as you lay them, it's a good idea to put in temporary forms. Drive sharpened stakes at 4-ft. or 5-ft. intervals along the excavation. The tops of the stakes should be at the level of the finished walk, and the sides should be just far enough from the edges of the walk to leave room for a 2×4 or a piece of plywood. For straight walks, nail 2×4s even with the top of the stakes to create a frame. If your walk is curved, bend strips of ¼-in. or ⅜-in. plywood and nail them to the stakes. Then, shovel soil against the outside of the forms to prevent the stone dust from spilling out under the 2×4s or the plywood.

If your walkway is on level ground, pitch it to eliminate standing water. A drop of ¼ in. per 1 ft. of width is enough to encourage runoff. For example, a 3-ft. wide walk should have one side ¾ in. higher than the other. Check the pitch with a level and adjust the height of the forms accordingly.

A bed for the bricks

Inside the forms, put down a 3-in. layer of stone dust followed by a 1-in. layer of sand. To distribute stone dust and sand evenly, you'll need to make two screeds (leveling boards). I cut lengths of 2×4s about 8 in. wider than the walk and notch each end so that the 2×4s hang inside the forms down to the top level of the stone dust or sand. (See photo on facing page.) I push the screed along the forms, which serve as rails, spreading and smoothing the stone dust or sand. To reduce settling, I compact the stone dust with a hand tamper (available at rental centers) before adding the sand. I don't compact the sand—bricklaying settles it into place.

Laying the bricks

This step is easy. To establish the pattern, I start at one corner of the walk and work across to the opposite edge. Then I set each brick firmly into the sand by tapping it down lightly with my hammer handle. Sometimes I crack a brick as I tap it. Since the crack will only get larger, I discard the brick without hesitation. I stop occasionally to make sure that the bricks are even with the top of the forms by laying a 2×4 across the walk. If I have trouble getting a brick to settle down into position, I slide it back and forth in the sand. I raise low bricks up to level by removing them and adding sand.

The author taps a brick into place in a basket weave pattern using the handle of a hammer. As he goes, he checks that the bricks are at the correct height by laying a straight edge, such as the level behind him, across the forms. He also checks that the pattern is in line using the square at his side.

No matter what pattern you choose, sooner or later you'll have to cut a brick. Use a tool called a brick-set chisel, which has a 4-in. wide blade. Mark the brick where you want to cut it by drawing a line on it with a small square and a pencil. Lay the brick on a piece of 2×4 or on the ground to cushion it. Set the brick-set chisel on the line and strike it with a hammer. Wear safety glasses; flying chips can injure unprotected eyes.

When you've finished laying the bricks, remove the forms and fill in along the edges with earth removed during excavation. If you ran your walk across a lawn, reset strips of the sod you pulled up along the edge of the walk. The last step is to throw a couple of shovelsful of sand on the walk and sweep it into the spaces between the bricks with a stiff broom.

Your walk can be used immediately. You can put in a walk in one day and entertain guests that night. □

Richard T. Kreh, Sr. is a masonry consultant in Frederick, Maryland.

A gracefully curving flight of low and wide flagstone steps provides safe and easy passage to and from the entrance of the author's old farmhouse. Setting the flagstone treads behind the Belgian-block facings visually emphasizes the edge of the steps and adds an attractive contrast.

Designing Outdoor Steps

Proper layout for a safe, comfortable stride

by Betty Ajay

Well-designed steps can be a valuable part of the landscape, and provide a pleasing and safe way to get from one place to another. Unfortunately, outdoor steps are too often poorly planned. This results in a pathway that's unattractive, and often hazardous, requiring the pedestrian to take giant strides or tiny steps to land squarely on the treads.

Designing steps isn't hard, however. While it does call for careful thought and a good understanding of the basics, it's well within the reach of any gardener. Even if you don't plan to install the steps yourself, knowing how to design them will help you work knowledgeably with a mason or a professional landscaper.

When I'm planning outdoor steps, I find it most practical to think of them in two categories: those that lead from the house to the garden, and those that connect two levels of land within the garden. Each of these situations has its own set of problems to be solved, but designing steps for either is based on establishing a correct ratio between the horizontal dimension of the step (the tread) and its vertical dimension (the riser).

Tread/riser ratio

Properly designed steps should enable you to go up and down without changing your normal stride. This means that a tall riser must be paired with a shallow tread, and a shorter riser with a deeper tread. When this general relationship is altered, the steps can be dangerous to walk on. Steps should allow you to pay more attention to the landscape, and less to where your feet are falling.

The dimensions most commonly used for steps in a professionally-designed landscape are a 6-in. riser with a 14-in. tread, a 5-in. riser with a 16-in. tread, or a 4-in. riser with an 18-in. tread. Steps such as these are comfortable to climb and pleasing to the eye. They will accommodate the change of grade in most gardens, with the exception of very steep sites. Steps of these dimensions won't have risers that are as high or treads that are as narrow as indoor steps, and with good reason. Indoor steps transplanted to the garden might be comfortable to walk on, but they will appear out of place because they're not in scale with the much larger dimensions of the outdoors.

No matter what dimensions you choose, you can use a simple formula to calculate a correct tread/riser relationship: twice the height of the riser plus the depth of the tread, the distance from front to back, should equal 26. This relationship can be modified, but only slightly, or else you'll compromise the safety and natural stride the steps afford.

Steps leading from house to garden

If your house has no porch or terrace outside the entrance, you should first design a platform that will extend immediately out from the threshold and connect with the steps. Make the platform a minimum depth of 4 ft., which is enough room for someone to open the door of the house without having to step back off the platform.

In most cases, the best choice for entrance steps is the lowest riser and broadest tread that will fit into the amount of space available. Such steps are easier to climb than those with high risers, and they more effectively ease the transition from the house to its surroundings.

To calculate the most suitable dimensions for a particular flight of steps, first measure the vertical distance between the threshold and the finished grade of the land to which the stairs are leading. Then sketch out various combinations of riser and tread dimensions, as shown in the bottom drawing at right. Since the last riser brings you to ground level, which is, in effect, a tread, there is always one less tread than there are risers.

The total depth of all the treads will add up to the horizontal distance to be traveled by the steps. By adding this to the depth of the platform, you'll know how far the steps will extend laterally from the house, a distance called the run.

For example, if your steps need to descend 3 ft. from a 4-ft.-deep threshold platform, you have several options. With a 6-in. riser and 14-in. tread, the drop would require six risers and five treads, and the steps would run a little less than 6 ft. A 4-in. riser and 18-in. tread would require nine risers and eight treads.

If your house is large and there's plenty of space for the flight of steps, you can build low, deep steps. A 4-in. riser and 18-in. tread usually looks best. But if your house is small or space is limited, steps of these dimensions may look too grand and take up too much room. In this case, try a 5-in. riser and 16-in. tread. I don't recommend using risers higher than 6 in. or treads narrower than 14 in. for steps leading from a house, unless steps of these dimensions just won't fit into the available space. If you must build steeper steps, remember that they're likely to look out of scale even with a very small house.

I'd encourage you to experiment on paper with different tread/riser measurements until you come up with a combination that will fit in the run. I also suggest that you mock up the steps before you commit the time and resources to building them. It's easy to do this by setting boards that are the depth of the treads on bricks or concrete blocks that are the height of the risers. Stand back and see how they look in relationship to the house. If you plan to try out the design by walking on the boards, make sure they're securely in place.

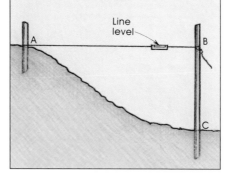

Measuring elevation change

1. To measure the change in elevation between two levels of land, drive a short stake into the ground at the highest point (A) and a tall stake at the lowest point (C).

2. Tie a line to the short stake, flush with the ground, and pull it taut out to the tall stake.

3. Place a line level on the line and move the line up and down gently against the tall stake until it's level.

4. Then fasten the line to the tall stake exactly where the line touches. The distance between B and C is the change in elevation. The distance between A and B is the horizontal dimension the steps will cover.

Once you've determined a comfortable tread/riser ratio, you'll need to decide on a proper width for your steps. This decision is really a matter of personal judgment—there are no hard and fast rules. But there are a few tricks of the trade that should help you. Low, broad entrance steps also should be wide enough to look in scale when viewed against the facade of the house. Given enough space, I like to make such steps a minimum of 5 ft. wide, enough room for two people to walk on them side by side. In many situations, I make them much wider. A 16-in.- or 18-in.-deep tread looks clumsy and heavy if it's crammed into a narrow space. On the other hand, a shallow tread, 12 in. for example, looks insubstantial if the step is too wide. A wide step accentuates the shallowness, and the result is a badly proportioned step.

Try out steps of different widths and keep experimenting with the dimensions until you arrive at a pleasing relationship among the height of the risers, the depth of the treads, the width of the steps and the length the steps will run.

Steps connecting levels within the garden

Wherever there is a major change in elevation between different levels of the garden, steps are the best way to join them. If the elevation change is minimal, you could make an inclined walkway instead. Steps are usually a better choice, however, since level surfaces are safer to walk on than slopes, and, by accentuating a change in grade, steps sharpen the lines of the entire landscape design.

Once you've decided where to place

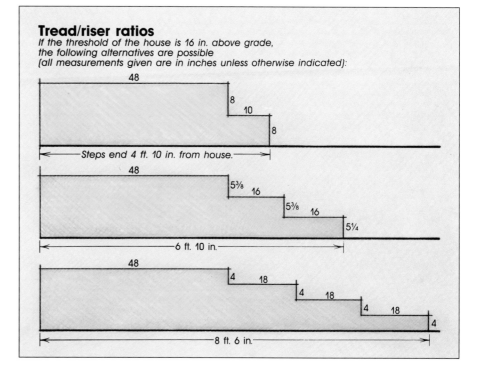

Tread/riser ratios
If the threshold of the house is 16 in. above grade, the following alternatives are possible (all measurements given are in inches unless otherwise indicated):

48   8 / 10 / 8
Steps end 4 ft. 10 in. from house.

48   5⅜ / 16 / 5⅜ / 16 / 5¼
6 ft. 10 in.

48   4 / 18 / 4 / 18 / 4 / 18 / 4
8 ft. 6 in.

the steps, you'll need to figure out a correct tread/riser ratio. First, measure the change in elevation covered by the steps, as shown in the top drawing on p. 13. Then you can figure out different tread/riser ratios in the same way as described for steps leading from the house to the garden. Use the formula given earlier: twice the riser plus the tread should equal 26. Work out various combinations that will span the grade change.

If this change of grade is slight, then a low riser and broad tread will work fine and provide a gentle transition. But a steep grade generally requires a higher riser and narrower tread in order to make the climb without an excessive number of steps. This is especially true where you need to connect two levels in the shortest amount of space.

But sometimes a steep flight of steps cutting straight up a slope can be difficult to climb, and unattractive as well. If your site is like this, then consider curving the steps or using platforms (landings) to break up the climb, as shown in the drawing at right. By increasing the run in this way, you can use a lower riser and broader tread, although you'll probably need to build a retaining wall on the uphill side of the stairs to hold back the earth.

Figuring out a suitable width for steps connecting garden levels is very similar to working out the width for steps from the house, as described earlier. In general, when the treads are deep, the steps should be wide. But low, broad steps joining two levels within a garden can be even wider than those leading from the house and still seem in scale with their surroundings. Without a house or other structure as a backdrop, the eye measures the steps against the sky and the expanse of the garden. This is especially true in larger gardens, with tall trees in view, but wide steps can also be used successfully to connect two levels in a smaller garden.

Choosing materials

First, decide if you will dry-lay the steps or set them in mortar. I think mortared steps, which have a more formal appearance, look better closer to the house, and dry-laid steps, which are lighter-looking and less formal, are more appropriate within the garden. Entrance steps should usually be set in mortar to stabilize them, since there is typically an abrupt change of grade between most houses and the immediately adjacent land.

Materials for dry-laid steps need to serve as both riser and tread, or as the riser and part of the tread. But if steps are set in mortar, you can use different materials for the riser and the tread. Flagstone treads with brick risers or risers of fieldstone or Belgian block make beautiful mortared steps. If Belgian block is available, masons often prefer it to fieldstone, because these small stone blocks are uniform in size and don't have to be selected and fitted as carefully as fieldstones.

Mortared steps—*Bricks* make quite attractive steps, both as riser and tread. Ordinary builder's bricks will absorb moisture, and in cold climates they'll eventually crack and crumble from freeze-thaw cycling (called spalling) if they're laid on a horizontal surface. So make sure you use hard-fired brick. (See p. 10 for more on choosing brick for walkways.) Hard-fired brick is available in a variety of colors, ranging from red to pale pink, from tan to black.

Flagstone, sometimes called bluestone, is probably one of the most versatile materials for treads. It's comparatively easy to handle, long-lasting and maintenance-free. Its pleasing blue-gray color blends well with all other colors in the garden. Purchase flagstone that's at least 1½ in. thick, although 2 in. thick is even better. The thicker stones make handsomer treads and are less liable to chip at the edges. One drawback to flagstone is its high cost, particularly where it's not readily available, but I still think it's a good value for the money.

Poured concrete is relatively inexpensive, but it has serious disadvantages when used to build landings and steps. In time, hairline cracks develop, particularly in cold climates, and even worse, the risers become water-stained. A stark expanse of concrete can appear rather harsh as well. Brushing the surface to give a textured appearance, or adding an attractive aggregate and exposing it through troweling will improve the look of the concrete, but the latter requires considerable skill. If you hire a mason to do the job, the cost will be about the same as if you used a more expensive material like flagstone.

Dry-laid steps—*Quarry stones* make excellent dry-laid steps, and installation consists of simply digging them into the grade. If there's a quarry in your vicinity, they can be ordered in precise dimensions; you can specify the exact tread and riser size you need. Order the stones 1 in. deeper than the tread depth and overlap them to hold them in place. Quarry stones are very heavy, and depending on size, it can take two people or more to muscle one into place.

Flat fieldstones, in theory, could be used in the same way as quarry stones, but it's almost impossible to find ones that are uniform enough in size to make safe and comfortable steps. However, thick, flat fieldstones do look attractive if the change in elevation is minimal and you need only a few steps. In this case, the stones' irregularity is unlikely to be hazardous.

Railroad ties, creosoted under pressure, are suitable for risers and the front part of treads. Ties measure approximately 8 in. by 8 in. and are 8 ft. long. Brick, flagstone, crushed stone or another tie is the material used most often to complete the depth of the tread. By varying the amount of the tie that's buried, you can make risers up to 8 in. high. By varying the width of the material used to fill in behind the tie, you can make the correct tread size for the riser you've chosen. □

Betty Ajay, a landscape designer, lives in Bethel, Connecticut.

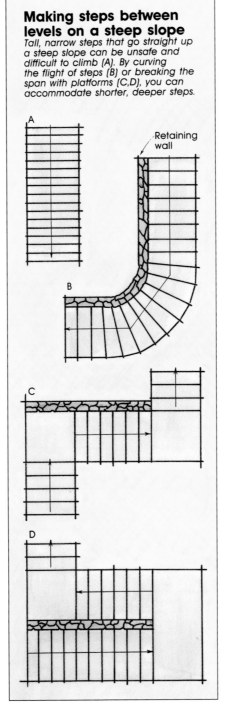

Making steps between levels on a steep slope
Tall, narrow steps that go straight up a steep slope can be unsafe and difficult to climb (A). By curving the flight of steps (B) or breaking the span with platforms (C,D), you can accommodate shorter, deeper steps.

A

Retaining wall

B

C

D

A narrow bed of low-growing plants near the edge of the porch acts as a visual barrier to prevent people from backing off the edge. Curving the path allowed the author to use lower steps without having them extend out too far from the entrance.

Steps for easy walking

After years of designing countless outdoor steps for clients, I finally decided that I couldn't ignore the entrance to my own house any longer. Until recently, my husband and I had been served well by the narrow flagstone porch along part of the front of the house and the stone steps leading from it to ground level. The massive steps, with their uneven surfaces, suited our old farmhouse and didn't pose an obstacle to walking when we and most of our friends were young and sure-footed. But as the years went by, our guests, much older now, arrived at the front door often out of breath from the steep climb. And for us, climbing the stairs with heavy bags of groceries had become more difficult.

I decided to redesign the entire approach to our house—the porch and steps, as well as a dilapidated stone path leading from the parking area to the steps. The new entrance had to be functional, and it had to mesh attractively with our house and land. The walk needed to be easy to travel on—as level as possible and wide enough for people to walk two abreast comfortably. The steps also had to be easy to climb, even when we or delivery people were carrying heavy packages.

I put much thought into the new plan, sketching and resketching different options until I was satisfied. I widened the porch to 8½ ft. I considered adding a railing to it and to the steps for safety, but decided that a railing just wouldn't look right with our 18th-century house. Instead, I incorporated an 18-in.-wide planting strip along the entire length of the porch, set in 1 ft. from the outside edge. Planted with low-growing holly (*Ilex*

crenata 'Helleri'), it creates a psychological barrier and keeps people away from the edge of the porch.

To make the steps easy to climb, I decided to use 4-in. risers and 18-in. treads. If I had run the steps straight out from the house, they would have extended out 12 ft., which would have overwhelmed our modest farmhouse. (The 3-ft. drop from the door to ground level required nine risers and eight treads of the above dimensions.) Fortunately, the entrance walk from the parking area is at the side of the house, so I could curve the steps around in an arc. Laid out in this way, their length wasn't objectionable. To make the

curve, the treads had to be wider at the outside of the arc and narrower at the inside, with the center remaining 18 in.

Since easy walking was my main concern, I broke up the 12-ft. run even further with a 3-ft.-long landing platform. This extends the steps even further and makes the change in levels less perceptible. At the foot of the steps, there is a short stretch of walk and then an additional drop in grade of 2 ft. with more low, broad steps (4-in. risers and 18-in. treads). Closer to the driveway, I've also added a tread and two risers to keep the walk even more level. Based on the natural slope of the land, one riser would have been enough, but one riser is hard to see and would trip the unwary. Next to the house, the steps are 8 ft. wide. There, they're in good proportion to the house and wide enough for a railing to be unnecessary.

The treads and the porch are made of flagstone. The monochromatic effect of the gray house and gray stone is quite pleasing. The fieldstone retaining walls that shore up the sides of the steps and the front and sides of the porch are also gray, and match the stone foundation of the house.

Belgian blocks form the risers. I had the masons fit the flagstones behind the blocks, rather than setting the flagstones on top of the blocks, as is usually done. This method of construction makes each riser more visible, and consequently the steps are safer. It also gives a decorative edge to the steps and makes the low risers appear less clumsy than they would have with just 2½ in. of Belgian block visible beneath the 2-in. flagstone tread.

The flagstones on the porch and the steps are laid in mortar, but those on the walk are dry-laid in stone dust. This was less expensive, and also avoided the formal look that a long flagstone path with mortar joints can lend to a country property. Since we used 2-in.-thick flagstones and carefully fitted the joints, the walk is almost as solid as if it were laid in mortar.   —B.A.

Two steps partway up the path help level out the rest of the walk. Two risers make the steps more visible than if just one had been used.

A Dry-Laid Paver Patio

Install a smooth, attractive surface for outdoor living

This patio serves as an outdoor gathering spot for relaxing and entertaining. It also acts as a transition space between the house and the surrounding garden. The author and her husband designed and installed this patio themselves, using concrete pavers which give the look of stone at a fraction of the cost.

by Mary Anne Cassin

utting in a patio behind our new house was a high priority. My husband and I spend a lot of time outdoors gardening, but every now and then we like to sit back, relax and admire the results of our labors. We also like to spend as much time as possible enjoying the Portland, Oregon, climate. Winters here are short, and the temperatures tend to remain above freezing. And summers are heavenly—consistently sunny but not hot or humid, ideal for dining and entertaining al fresco.

My husband is a landscape contractor and I am a landscape architect, so we had plenty of background in the technical skills that would be required for patio construction. These skills are not out of reach for the average home gardener, however. You can install a patio like ours if you do some research into materials and construction techniques (see Resources on p. 18).

Choosing a location and design

A flat spot on the north side of the house, accessible through the living room's French doors, seemed the natural spot to locate a patio. The yard and gardens frame this area on three sides. In a colder climate, a north-facing patio might not be usable for several months of the year, but because of our mild weather, we're able to use our patio year-round.

When deciding how big to make the patio, we considered the activities we wanted to take place there. We anticipated dinner parties and large gatherings of friends. We wanted room for a table and six chairs, with plenty of circulation space around them. We started by sketching things out on paper, including a rough drawing of the house and the yard and compass points. Laying out the future patio with stakes and string before we ordered any materials (see Estimating the quantities on p. 18) gave us a better feel for the shape, size and location we'd chosen.

Paving materials

We began our search for a paving material by considering the traditional alternatives. None of them met our needs. We ruled out concrete and asphalt because a patio as large as ours (20 ft. × 30 ft.) would have required professional finish detailing to break up the monotony of these materials. Brick is attractive, relatively inexpensive and durable, but it can be quite slippery in this climate because moss thrives on it. We liked the idea of a stone surface, but the cost turned out to be prohibitive, as much as $8 to $10 per sq. ft. Our budget for the 600-sq.-ft. patio was $2,000.

We finally decided on precast concrete paving stones. These paving units are widely used in Canada and Europe, but haven't been readily available in the United States until recently. A variety of paver styles and colors is available. The one we chose

is called a "Roman paver." It has been tumbled, which roughens the edges, so it really does look like stone, especially when it's wet. Also, for some reason, moss doesn't grow on the

A closer look at the patio gives a better idea of the sort of cutting required to fit a diagonal pattern into a rectangular space. The basalt cobble edging that Cassin and her husband used along the flower beds serves as a rustic complement to the more formal pavers.

Cutaway view of a paver patio

The keys to successful dry-laid patio installation: proper preparation of the subbase and sand bed, and installation of an edging to contain the pavers. Cassin and her husband excavated the patio area, filled the low spots with crushed rock and put down a 2-in. bed of sand directly on the subbase. (Gardeners in colder regions may have to excavate deeper and add a 3-in. to 8-in. base of crushed rock before laying sand.) Basalt cobbles and pressure-treated 2 x 6s form the edging.

Pressure-treated 2 x 6 edging
18-in. rebar
Basalt cobble edging
Concrete pavers
2-in. bed of sand
Compacted subbase excavated to 2% slope, with crushed rock used to fill low spots
Concrete footing for cobbles

pavers' surfaces; it only grows in the cracks. Finally, concrete pavers are meant to be dry-laid (laid on a bed of sand), so we didn't have to bother with the mess of mortar.

The cost met our objective: the material price (delivered) was only $2 per sq. ft., for a total cost of about $1,200. And we don't have to worry about durability. The pavers are manufactured to withstand a pressure of 3500 lbs./sq. in. With proper base

preparation, they can be used for roadway construction.

Installation

Successful installation of a dry-laid paver patio lies in proper preparation of the foundation on which the pavers rest. Accurate measurement and attention to construction details are important as you work on the layers of the sandwich: subbase (the ground beneath the patio), base (a layer of crushed rock), sand bed and pavers. Just as important is the edging, which must be put in place around the perimeter of the patio before you begin paving. Because the pavers are dry-laid, they would soon shift without an edging to contain them.

Establishing elevation— We wanted the patio to follow existing grades as much as possible so that it would look like it belonged in its surroundings. We also made sure that the finished surface had a minimum slope of 2% (a drop of 6 in. over a 25-ft. run) so water would drain off away from the house foundation. The patio could have had a greater slope than this, but your eye can determine a definite pitch at slopes of 4% or more. The closer the patio is to a house or other level surfaces, the more obvious the pitch. Our patio appeared level until we built a deck next to it; now the 2% slope is quite distinct.

We used a string level (also called a line level— a small level hooked onto a length of string) hung between stakes to mark out the elevation of the patio. We drove the stakes into the corners and studied the "givens" of the site. We knew what elevation we wanted the future deck to have, so we started by leveling the strings at that height. We also knew that the patio should slope to the west, in keeping with the existing grade. Since our patio was 30 ft. wide in the direction of the slope, it had to have a minimum drop of 0.6 ft. to achieve the required 2%

grade (30 ft. × .02 = 0.6 ft. or 7\%6 in). To arrive at this slope, we dropped the string 7\%6 in. down the stakes at the low end of the patio. We used the strings as guides to determine the depth of the subbase excavation.

Installing the edging—Although the manufacturers' brochures suggest preparing the subbase next, we decided to install the edging first to limit soil disturbance along the edge of the patio and to minimize damage to the lawn. The edging material can take many different forms: concrete curbs, wooden boards, strips of PVC or steel bands. We chose a combination of stone and lumber.

We used split basalt cobbles as a prominent edge along the rock garden and annual beds. We mortared these in place on a 6 in. × 6 in. concrete footing (you may need a deeper footing in a colder climate). We wanted to minimize the visibility of the edging around the rest of the patio to give it a more open feel. Here we used pressure-treated 2 × 6s, setting them ½ in. below finished patio grade so that the deck, lawn and surround-ing plants would conceal them later.The wood is held in place by concrete-reinforcement bars ("rebars"), which we purchased in 10-ft. lengths from a lumberyard. We cut the rebars into 18-in. pieces with a hack saw and pounded them in place on the outside of the wood every 5 ft. or so.

Preparing the subbase—The first step in preparing the subbase was to determine how deep to dig. To do this, we added the depth of the sand layer to be spread over the subbase (2 in.) to the thickness of the pavers. Then we subtracted this total from finished grade to find the elevation of the subbase.

Because our climate is mild and because we expected only foot traffic on our patio, it wasn't necessary to have any special base between the subbase and the sand bed. In colder climates, though, you may need to excavate 3 in. to 8 in. and fill the area with a base of crushed rock to reduce the chances of frost heave and settling. Check with the paver manufacturer or a local contractor to determine what sort of preparation is recommended in your area.

As we dug, we checked the depth at 6-in. intervals by measuring the distance from the ground to a string set at finished grade. We walked along the string with a tape measure and marked the high and low points with chalk, then moved the string and repeated the process. In this way, we

were able to get a good idea of the size and shape of the bumps and the dips. We leveled the bumps with our shovels and we filled in low spots with *crushed*, ¾-in.-minus rock (a mix of pieces no larger than ¾ in.). Only crushed rock will compact to the density required to provide a firm surface.

My husband and I spent the better part of a week, putting in a couple of hours every day, excavating and filling the low spots. We lifted the sod with spades (if you have to lift a lot of turf, consider renting a sod cutter) and removed the soil below with a flat, square-point shovel, checking the level as we went. (Call the electric and water utility companies before you begin to

---

RESOURCES

There are many concrete paver manu-facturers and distributors in the U.S. and Canada. Readers in most areas will find them listed in the yellow pages of the phone book under Concrete Products. Many manufacturers are represented by one or both of the following industry associations which can refer you to the member nearest you and provide basic information on paver specifications and installation:

Concrete Paver Institute (a division of the National Concrete Masonry Association), 2302 Horse Pen Rd., Herndon, VA 22071. 703-435-4900.

National Precast Concrete Association, 825 E. 64th St., Indianapolis, IN 46220. 800-428-5732.

---

be sure that your digging won't damage underground cables or pipes.)

Once we arrived at the proper elevation, we compacted the subbase. We initially thought we could do a good enough job with a hand tamper, but we found that a motorized plate compactor (available from most rental companies) did a much better job. A plate compactor is noisy (ear plugs are a must) and heavy, but simple to operate. We ran it over the surface several times in each direction to be sure the material was adequately compacted.

It's important to get the subbase as level as possible (within ¼ in.) because the pavers will eventually settle to conform to the subbase's contours. The plate compactor did not radically change the level of the excavation, but it did cause some uneven settling. We checked the grade again and added more gravel where necessary.

Laying the pavers—The paving itself took only two days, though they were long days. First, we spread the layer of sand on which the pavers rest. Our manufacturer recommended 2 in.; others may suggest as little as 1 in. We then screeded the sand (leveled it with a straight edge). We built a special screed—two 10-ft.-long 2 × 4s bolted together in the middle—to accommodate our large patio area. We notched the screed on either end so that it hung down to the desired level from the edging. Where we used the cobbles as an edging material, a board placed inside the stones served as a level guide.

It had already been a long day by the time we finished smoothing the sand. We pushed on because once the sand is down, it must not be disturbed until the pavers are in place, and we have pets who would have loved that huge litter box. So we spread all the sand and laid most of the pavers in one day, finishing up by floodlight at 11:30 p.m. We laid long planks over the rows of exposed sand to keep our pets at bay for the night.

Depending on your selection of pavers, there are several patterns to choose from: running bond, herring-bone and basket weave, among others. We chose a pattern that looks like a series of pinwheels, and set it on a diagonal to make it more dynamic. We bordered this pattern on all four sides with a row of pavers set perpendicular to the edge.

Placing the pavers wasn't difficult, but keeping them in line within the pattern was a little tricky. We started in a corner where the angle was exactly 90°, and kept a close eye on spacing, but we still found it necessary to start over more than once. The task was complicated by the need to leave a ⅛-in. gap between each paver on all sides. (Some manufacturers make pavers with built-in spacers.)

My husband had been skeptical about the wisdom of choosing a pattern that required the cutting of some 200 pavers, but the ease of using a brick saw allayed his concerns. The saw, which we also rented locally, is mounted on legs, so we could work standing up. Because the saw operates with a diamond blade under a constant stream of water, cutting the pavers was noisy and messy, but it was precise and quick. (Remember to wear safety goggles and ear plugs when operating a brick saw.) We were able to cut all the pavers (using chalk to mark the cuts), place them and apply the finishing touches in time to dine on the patio the second day.

After placing the last pavers, we ran the plate compactor over the entire surface twice in both directions. This was horribly loud because of the hard surface. It brought out those neighbors who had not already been inspecting our progress.

The last part was easy and very satisfying. We swept dry sand over the surface (a wheelbarrow load is all we needed) to fill in the gaps between the pavers, and arranged the furniture and potted plants. We thought about christening the patio with a bottle of champagne but decided to drink it instead.

Maintenance

Our patio is now three years old, and has lived up to our expectations in every way. We are happy to see the moss starting to fill in the cracks in the shadier corners, and we have fun experimenting with different arrangements of potted plants. Weeds do pop up in the cracks now and then, but an occasional spot spraying with Safer's Sharpshooter gets rid of them. The only other maintenance required is an annual spring replenishment of sand swept into the cracks to replace that washed away by winter rains.

We haven't noticed any significant settling or heaving, but if and when we do, repair will be simple. Since the pavers aren't mortared in place, all we have to do is lift the affected area, correct the base and re-lay the pavers.

The patio now looks as though it has always been there. With a treated hemlock deck connecting the patio to the house, we've created the perfect outdoor room from which to view our garden. □

Mary Anne Cassin is a landscape architect with the Portland, Oregon, Park Bureau.

Photos: Kenneth E. Meyer

Dry-laid pavers rest on a bed of sand. The author and her husband leveled the sand to the correct depth with a screed, which they made by bolting two 10-ft. 2 × 4s together. They notched the ends of the screed so that it hung down to the correct depth from the edging.

Cassin and her husband chose a pinwheel pattern set diagonally within a frame of pavers laid long side perpendicular to the edge. They used cardboard to space the pavers the recommended ⅛ in. apart until they discovered that the pavers were smashing the cardboard flat. They switched to ⅛-in. drill bits to finish the job.

Once all of the pavers were laid, the patio was compacted, using a motorized plate compactor. Although heavy and noisy, it made compacting easy. The final job was sweeping a wheelbarrow load of dry sand into the cracks.

Building Your Own Retaining Wall

Professional techniques ensure strength and longevity

by Dale Johnson

Timber retaining walls are handsome and useful garden structures. They break slopes into terraces, where plants can grow on display. They let you add level ground to your property. They lend character to patios, entryways and foundation plantings.

But building a timber wall is more than stacking wood. Good construction requires the right timbers and fasteners, a solid foundation, regularly spaced anchors, and drainage. I've been building timber walls professionally for 18 years, long enough to know that they can be designed for almost any site and taste, and long enough to learn what makes a wall look good and last.

Can you build your own timber retaining walls? You can, if you're comfortable with tape measure, drill, chainsaw and carpenter's level, and if you don't mind hard work with a shovel. I'm not saying that you can build a wall anywhere. Tall slopes take experience. I retain them with several walls, built like a flight of stairs. Every "step" depends for solidity on the step below it, and construction is tricky. I recommend that you stick to slopes you can retain with one wall, and that's what I'll talk about here. The drawing at right shows the basics of construction. So long as you keep these in mind, the design of your own wall is up to you.

Timbers—Use pressure-treated timbers. In contact with soil, they resist rot and insects and remain sound far longer than timbers of any wood reputed to be decay-resistant, and far longer than timbers treated with wood preservatives by painting, soaking or hot-dipping. In pressure treatment, wood preservative is forced deep into the timber, protecting most if not all of the wood. I prefer pressure-treated pine timbers because I've found that pine absorbs wood preservative right to the core, while other woods often do not. Pressure-treated pine timbers should last 30 years or more. I've checked retaining walls that I installed 13 years ago and found the timbers as good as new. Timbers treated by painting, soaking or hot-dipping absorb preservative on the surface. When the wood cracks and checks, insects and fungi move into the unprotected core, and the timbers are shot in ten years.

I use penta-treated and CCA-treated timbers. "Penta" stands for pentachlorophenol, a clear preservative that darkens wood but otherwise preserves its tan or gray color. CCA (composed of compounds of chromium, copper and arsenic) leaves wood with a greenish tinge, which fades with weathering. In my area, CCA-treated timbers are cheaper than penta-treated timbers, but I prefer penta because of the natural look. Freshly treated penta timbers are often soaking wet with preservative. You must handle them with caution—wear gloves, avoid prolonged skin contact, wash well when you stop working, wear safety goggles to keep chips and sawdust out of your eyes, and avoiding inhaling the sawdust. You must also give the timbers time to dry before you plant. Penta vapors stunt and kill plants. I recommend waiting a month before planting near a new retaining wall of penta-treated timbers. The compounds in CCA timbers bind chemically to the wood and pose fewer hazards. Wear gloves and goggles and avoid breathing the sawdust. You can plant as soon as construction ends.

Though timbers come in several dimensions that are suitable for walls, I recommend 8-ft.-long 5x6s. They're less expensive than 6x6s, and faster to build with than 5x5s. I lay the timbers with the 5-in. sides horizontal, so my walls go up 6 in. at a time. I choose the best-looking side for the face of a wall, but with only two sides to pick from, I sometimes have to use one that's knotty and split. I save the best-looking timbers for the top of the wall, where two faces show. For patios and walks, where I need one extra-good-looking face, I use 5x5s or 6x6s because they give me four sides to choose from.

Foundation—Timber retaining walls need solid foundations. If the soil settles or

Backfill with topsoil behind top two timber courses, and crown topsoil so runoff goes over wall.

36-in. length of ½-in. rebar

Dig trench in steps, bury 3 ft. of each course, and overlap timber below 2 ft. or more.

Construction basics of a timber retaining wall

shifts, so will the wall. On sandy or clay soils, I compact the footing before building. On loose fill, or soil with a lot of organic matter, I compact the footing, then spread and compact a 6-in. layer of gravel. I use ¾-minus gravel—which is everything from ¾-in. pieces to dust—because it packs well. For compacting, I use a plate tamper and muscle power, or rent a gas-powered tamper.

Illustrations: Vince Babak

Timber retaining walls demand careful construction. If the bottom timbers shift or settle, so will the wall. Author Johnson digs a trench for them, and levels and compacts the soil, as shown here.

Johnson lays the bottom timbers in the trench, tamps soil beside them to hold them in place, drills a ½-in.-dia. hole 2 ft. from each end, and drives a 36-in. length of ½-in. rebar through each hole to resist the pressure of soil behind the wall.

Timber walls need good drainage. Johnson installs 4-in.- to 6-in.-dia. perforated pipe along the footing and shovels 1½-in. gravel against the timbers.

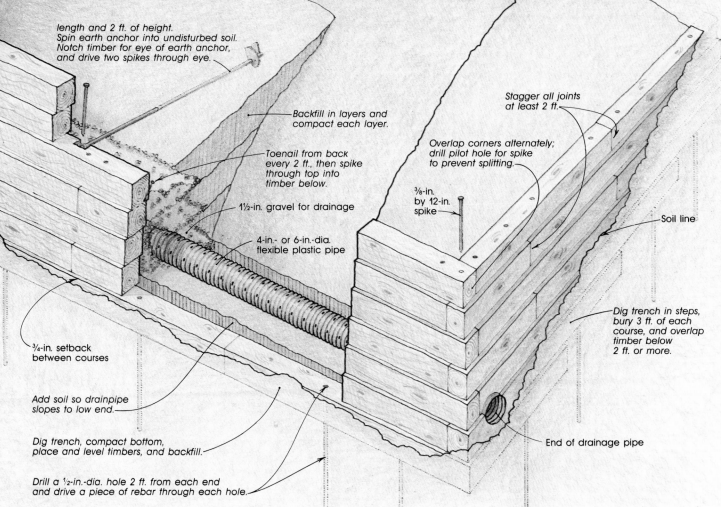

length and 2 ft. of height.
Spin earth anchor into undisturbed soil.
Notch timber for eye of earth anchor,
and drive two spikes through eye.

Backfill in layers and compact each layer.

Toenail from back every 2 ft., then spike through top into timber below.

1½-in. gravel for drainage

4-in.- or 6-in.-dia. flexible plastic pipe

Stagger all joints at least 2 ft.

Overlap corners alternately; drill pilot hole for spike to prevent splitting.

⅜-in. by 12-in. spike

Soil line

Dig trench in steps, bury 3 ft. of each course, and overlap timber below 2 ft. or more.

¾-in. setback between courses

Add soil so drainpipe slopes to low end.

Dig trench, compact bottom, place and level timbers, and backfill.

Drill a ½-in.-dia. hole 2 ft. from each end and drive a piece of rebar through each hole.

End of drainage pipe

Construction starts with a trench. Lay out the trench with stakes and string, and dig carefully to avoid disturbing the underlying soil. Be sure the bottom is level. I check as I go with a carpenter's level along the trench and a torpedo level across the trench. Dig the trench deep enough so the first timbers will be entirely below ground level (remember to dig 6 in. deeper if you're going to add gravel). Make the trench at least 10 in. wide so you don't have to contend with dirt spilling where the timbers go. Compact the trench, recheck the level, and adjust by shaving the high spots and compacting additional dirt in the low spots.

If you're working on a slope, you'll have to break the trench into steps. Look over the site, and start digging at the lowest point. Extend the trench until the working end is well below ground level and you can end with a good length of timber, 2 ft. at least. Lay timbers in the trench and start digging again, one step up—hold the bottom of the new trench level with the top of the timbers. Lap the next timber several feet over the last timber below, and make sure at least 3 ft. of the other end is below ground level.

When I lay the bottom timbers, I make

Toenailing and spiking timbers

Tilting the wall toward the slope makes it strong. Johnson sets each course of timbers ¾ in. back from the course below.

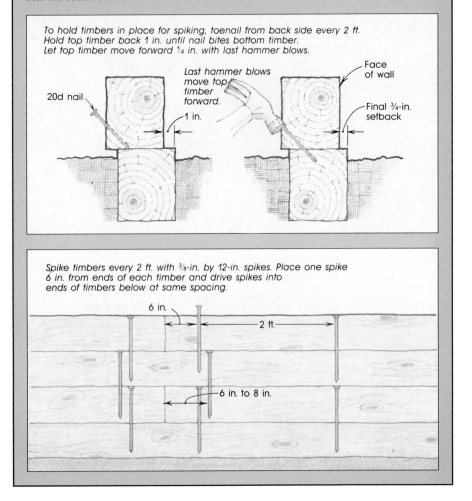

To hold timbers in place for spiking, toenail from back side every 2 ft. Hold top timber back 1 in. until nail bites bottom timber. Let top timber move forward ¼ in. with last hammer blows.

20d nail

Last hammer blows move top timber forward.

1 in.

Face of wall

Final ¾-in. setback

Spike timbers every 2 ft. with ⅜-in. by 12-in. spikes. Place one spike 6 in. from ends of each timber and drive spikes into ends of timbers below at same spacing.

6 in.

2 ft.

6 in. to 8 in.

sure they're solidly bedded and level, and then I pin them to the ground. Lay the timbers in the trench, line them up straight, and whack them hard several times with a sledgehammer to bed them firmly. Then check them for level. If you can't get a timber level with the sledgehammer, roll it out of the trench and dig or fill as needed. When all the timbers are level, shovel soil on both sides of them and tamp it carefully, making sure none creeps under the timbers. Then bore ½-in.-dia. holes in each timber, 2 ft. from the ends, and pound a 30-in. to 36-in. length of ½-in. rebar (the steel rod used to reinforce concrete) in each hole. When all the rebar is in, check the timbers again for level. If they're off, tap them with a sledgehammer. Be finicky. The first course of timbers is the foundation of all your work from here on up.

Laying up the wall—Lay up the timbers one course at a time, staggering them so each one spans two below it. Set each course back ¾ in. from the one below it. This setback tilts the wall slightly, so it leans into the slope and offers more resistance to the pressure of soil, water and ice than a vertical wall would. You can build timber walls without a setback, but if they're taller than 2 ft. you'll need engineering help.

I cut timbers with a gas-powered chainsaw. The more horsepower the better—an underpowered saw slows down, making the chain hard to guide. Mark timbers for cutting on adjacent sides. I prefer to cut with the back of the timber facing me—chainsaws tear wood on the side of the timber you're facing, and I want the face of the wall to look as good as possible. Here's a tip when you're butting timbers end-to-end and the joint is slightly crooked: Just run the chainsaw down the joint, shaving a bit off each timber, and you'll get a perfect match. Take care with a chainsaw. Wear safety glasses and gloves, stand on firm footing, and keep the blade outside the line of your body so a kickback won't hit you.

As you set each timber in place, nail it to keep it from moving until you can spike it. I toenail every 2 ft. on the back side into the timber below with 20d ring-shank nails (they often go by the name "pole-barn nails"). Start each nail a good 2 in. up the timber to allow for the setback, and hold the timber about 1 in. back from the timber below until the nail begins to bite (see the drawing at left). As you drive the nail home, the timber will move forward ¼ in., leaving you with a ¾-in. setback.

When you finish a course, spike it. I use ⅜-in. by 12-in. spikes. You can use 10-in. spikes and save 2 in. of work, but I like the extra holding power of the longer ones. Spikes come in 50-lb. boxes of roughly a hundred that cost about $30. To drive spikes, you need a maul—a sort of mini-sledgehammer. If you've never swung one, be prepared to discover some new muscles. Use an 8-lb. or 10-lb. maul, and practice before you start. When you're spiking, straddle the wall or stand alongside it. Don't hammer facing the wall—if you swing short of the spike, you're liable to mash the timber where the damage will show. If you find spiking too strenuous, you can ease the work by drilling a pilot hole for each spike to the timber below. Spikes sometimes split timbers at the ends. The damage matters only on the top course of a wall, where it would show. I always drill pilot holes for the top course.

Spike each timber 6 in. to 8 in. from each end, and 6 in. to 8 in. from each end of the two timbers below it. If you happen to hit a spike in the timber below, cut off the stalled spike with a hacksaw, move over an inch or two, and start a new spike. If a spike wanders and pops out the back of the timber, just drive it flush with the top of the timber, move over an inch or two, and drive another spike. If the spike wanders out the front of the timber, get the biggest crowbar you can find and pull it out. (This is a lot of work.) Then re-spike, taking account of how the first spike wandered.

Anchoring—To resist the pressure of soil, water and ice, the wall must be tied into the soil behind it at regular intervals. I reinforce my walls with earth anchors, which are steel contraptions with an auger at one end that you spin into undisturbed soil, and an eye at the other end that you fasten to the wall. They cost about $10 apiece. You need one every 8 ft. along a wall for every 2 ft. of height, placed in the middle of a timber. I install earth anchors with the same big crowbar I use to pull wandering spikes. Slip the crowbar through the eye and spin the auger into the soil. I angle the anchor so the eye comes to rest on the back edge of the timber. Then I push the eye aside an inch or two, notch the timber, push the eye into the notch, and secure it with two or three spikes. You should spin the auger at least 3 ft. into undisturbed soil. If the eye won't reach the wall, you have to cable it to an eyebolt in the wall (see the drawing at right). I use forged eyebolts; the eye is a complete circle and can't pull open. If you're working with disturbed dirt, such as fill from an excavation, you'll need engineering help to anchor the wall properly and a building permit before you start.

I anchor the ends of a wall by turning the courses back into the slope (see the drawing on p. 21). You can choose the angle of the corner to suit your taste and the slope. Prepare trenches for the end

walls as you did for the main wall, and set the bottom timbers the same way as before. The end walls should go up at the same time as the face wall. Each course of the end wall should cut into the slope at least 3 ft. Extend the trench in stairsteps to make room.

Drainage—When you've set three or four courses, start providing for drainage. You want water behind the wall to be able to escape freely, both to minimize pressure on the wall and to discourage insects and decay. I use gravel and 6-in.-dia. flexible perforated plastic pipe for drainage. I look over the site, decide which end of the wall the pipe should drain toward, and pack dirt behind the wall to slope in that direction. I carve an exit hole for the pipe in two timbers of the end wall. Then I lay the pipe on the dirt, and cover it with 1½-in. gravel.

For walls less than 2 ft. tall, and taller walls that have little water to contend with, I just drill 1½-in.-dia. weep holes

through the timbers just above the foundation course.

Backfill behind the wall after each course or two. First shovel gravel against the wall to maintain drainage to the foundation. Then add soil behind the gravel and compact the soil. When the last two courses are in place, backfill with topsoil and grade it carefully so it rises above the top timbers. You want runoff to go over the wall, not pool behind it.

Before you start—Stretch your imagination before you build. Walls can jog, step up, turn and turn again. You can set stairs in them, straight ahead, on an angle, or turning. Take your time planning. Draw the site and make overlays with tracing paper to compare alternative designs. The happier you are with your plan, the happier you'll be when you finish building. □

Dale Johnson's company, Environmental Landforms, in Minnetonka, Minnesota, specializes in timber retaining walls.

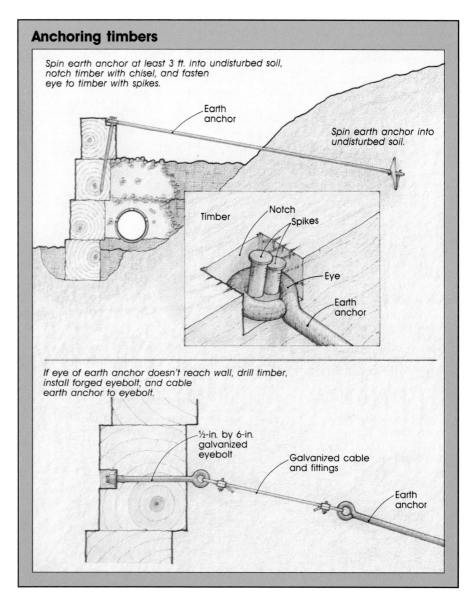

Anchoring timbers

Spin earth anchor at least 3 ft. into undisturbed soil, notch timber with chisel, and fasten eye to timber with spikes.

Earth anchor

Spin earth anchor into undisturbed soil.

Timber

Notch

Spikes

Eye

Earth anchor

If eye of earth anchor doesn't reach wall, drill timber, install forged eyebolt, and cable earth anchor to eyebolt.

½-in. by 6-in. galvanized eyebolt

Galvanized cable and fittings

Earth anchor

Building a Dry-Stone Retaining Wall

Carefully lapped layers look best, last longer

by Jim Sylvester

Of the structures we use to shape the landscape, few are more evocative than a stone retaining wall. The material and the construction methods are about as basic as you can get, as is the result: a mass of earth held in place by a stack of stones. Yet each wall has character. The stones—all different shapes, sizes and colors—supply a measure of this. But you have only to compare a pile of stones with a wall of stones to understand that most of the character is put there by the builder.

Transforming a pile of stones into a wall is hard work, but very satisfying. I've built miles of stone walls over the past eight years and still find it rewarding. (Be-

ing well paid for it has helped, too.) It's a project well within the reach of anyone with patience and the willingness to suffer a few sore muscles. I'll explain the structure of a dry-laid stone retaining wall and the methods I use to make one. The drawing and text on the facing page explain what goes into a wall. The photos above and on pp. 26-27 show details of building a fairly typical wall. The clients had cut into a low hill to widen their driveway, so I made a curving, 70-ft.-long wall, from 1 ft. to 5 ft. high, to hold the hillside.

Building a wall

Along their length, my walls follow the lay of the land, rising and falling with the slopes. If a slope is so steep that the stones

Author Sylvester builds his walls stair-step fashion. Above, he carefully positions a face stone.

slide off one another, you'll need to lay the wall in dug-out steps so that the courses will be at a shallower angle. I've never encountered this problem.

Across its width, however, the wall must rest on a level surface. On a big job, I make sure the backhoe operator excavates a level surface to the depth required for the pea-gravel foundation; on a small job, I do it myself with a pick and shovel. Our soil is either clay or gravel, neither of which requires tamping before the pea gravel is spread, though looser soil might.

Base stones establish the line of the wall. For straight walls, I lay base stones along a stretched string. I align curved walls by eye. If you don't trust your eye, lay out the curve with something flexible, like a garden hose. I always lay out at least 10 ft. of base stones ahead of where

(Text continues on p. 26.)

A dry-laid retaining wall

Engineering—Simple as a dry-laid retaining wall is, its engineering has to be sound. As the drawing shows, a good wall is carefully assembled of overlapping layers of stones infilled with smaller rocks and gravel. It must be massive enough to contain the weight of the soil behind it, and porous enough to allow moisture to drain—wet soil creeps and trapped water builds up considerable pressure. It should be as wide at its base as it is tall, with the most massive stones placed in the bottom layers. I angle the face of the wall toward the bank, creating a kind of buttress. The higher the wall, the greater the slope. For a wall 4 ft. high, with the bank level with the top of the wall, I'll go 15°

to 20°. If the bank slopes up from the wall, I'll angle the face back more. You can build a dry-laid wall of any size, but if you build much over 5 ft. or 6 ft. high, you'll need huge stones and heavy equipment to move them.

The stones—You can use almost any kind of flat stones. Round stones don't work well—even if you pile them up, you can't overlap layers, so they don't hold together. I use a mica schist called Goshen stone, quarried in Goshen, Massachusetts, which is a layered (sedimentary) stone with a lot of silvery mica in it. It's straight-grained and easy to split into thinner stones.

Dry-walling stones are cheaper than flagging stones or cut stones. The quarriers just bring big slabs down from the quarry, chop

them up with huge jackhammers, screen out the debris and scoop the stones onto the trucks. You take what you get. If you're fortunate, you'll get good building stones, needing little shaping with the hammer—you can just set them on the wall. A job will go twice as fast with a good load as with a bad one.

Traditionally, stone has been sold by the cubic yard, but because of trucking costs, some quarries now sell it by the ton. Last summer, stone cost me $35 a cubic yard plus shipping. A cubic yard of Goshen stone weighs roughly 1½ tons, and a 14-yard truckload will make a retaining wall about 3 ft. to 4 ft. high and 40 ft. long. (The formula is [length of wall x height] ÷ 25 = amount of stone in cubic yards.)

Section through completed wall

6. Cap stones

5. Fill stones

4. Tie stones

3. Face stones

2. Base stones

1. Foundation

Angle face of wall toward bank.

Width at base equals height of wall.

Level pea-gravel front to back.

1. The foundation—A concrete retaining wall needs a footing sunk beneath the frost line to keep frost heaving from cracking or destroying it. A dry-laid wall needs only a shallow pad of pea gravel (½-in. to ¾-in. stone). When the ground heaves, the pea gravel cushions the stones above. If they do move, they slide on one another and then fall back into place when the heaving subsides. I use 2 in. of pea gravel under walls a foot or so high; taller walls get an inch of gravel for each foot in height.

2. Base stones—These are the first stones placed and they form the first course of the wall's face. I select them from the largest and heaviest stones in the load, looking for ones with flat, parallel surfaces top and bottom and a nice face. For variety, I'll occasionally use a big stone with an unusual shape in the base course, but that increases the amount of chinking needed.

3. Face stones—Face stones give the wall its character. They can be of any size, with flat, parallel surfaces top and bottom and a good, flat edge for the face. The best face stones are wider at the front than at the back, so the ends of adjacent stones will fit tightly along the face. This makes for less chinking and, to my eye, a nicer-looking wall.

4. Tie stones—These long stones stretch from the face nearly to the bank and help bind the

wall together. For a wall 4 ft. to 5 ft. high, I try to place tie stones every other course or so, and every 4 ft. to 5 ft. along the run. If you can't find a stone that will bridge front to back, span the distance with two long stones set side by side, then lay a nice big one on top of them.

5. Fill stones—The stones you can't use for anything else fill the body of the wall behind the face. Though they aren't visible in the finished wall, it's important to lay them with some care. Try to get big ones near the bottom and—this is crucial—overlap the layers to tie everything together. I angle the fill at the back slightly down toward the bank, to make sure that the wall is leaning into the hillside.

6. Cap stones—The only stones that show on top of the wall are the cap stones. You'll need a variety of thicknesses to make this final course even on top. Cap stones can be as narrow as 6 in. to 8 in., or they can be wider for looks or to accommodate potted plants. You'll probably have to do some shaping with a hammer to get the caps to fit together with minimal gaps on top. I like to mortar the cap stones, particularly the narrower ones, to keep them in place if kids (or adults) walk on them. If you don't want to mortar them in, select good-size stones that fit together without a lot of chinking and whose weight will hold them in place. —J.S.

Illustrations: Gary Williamson

A section of wall begins with placement of the base stones. Here, Sylvester and his assistant lever a big base stone into place with heavy pry bars.

As the wall rises, Sylvester regularly adds tie stones that stretch from the face across the fill to the bank.

I'm building up the wall. Sometimes for shorter walls, I'll lay out all the base stones at once. Big pry bars and a heavy sledge are essential for moving these stones. I also drag them with a winch, or roll them on pieces of large-diameter pipe.

Lay some face stones next. Making sure to overlap joints, build a sort of stair that steps down from the beginning of the wall. Sometimes I'll find a stone that works best farther along the base and then need to find stones to fit in between. To angle the face of the wall back, I set the face of each course back just a smidgeon from that of the previous course. I like to put a biggish chunk here and there in the face, just for the visual effect.

I begin to lay fill stones when I see opportunities to layer them over and under any face stones that protrude in back. I may build up 1½ ft. to 2 ft. of face at the highest point before laying any fill stones. By then I've picked through the pile and begun to separate some of the fill from the face stones.

The most important thing to remember as you continue to lay up the wall is to overlap the stones throughout. On the face, stagger the joints by at least 3 in. to 4 in. (You may need to cut a bit off a rock to stagger the joints, or to fit it to a space. See the box below for how to do this.) Where the joints of several courses are unavoidably close together, span them if possible with a long piece. Layer the fill, set in tie stones regularly and take advantage of any chance to layer fill over the back side of a face stone. Try to keep the face and fill stones as level as possi-

On the rock pile

Tools—You don't need many tools to build a stone wall. Leaning against the wall in the photo at left, from left to right, are a 5-lb. sledge, a yardstick, a small pry bar, two large pry bars and a large sledge. In front, a brick hammer rests on a 3-lb. sledge.

I use the brick hammer and the lighter sledges for shaping stones. The larger the stone, the bigger the hammer. I also use a variety of cold chisels, which aren't shown here, for splitting stones. I move big stones with the large sledge or with the big pry bars, which weigh about 15 lb. each and have one chisel-pointed end—I jam the chisel point into the ground and pry the stone over. You can also move fairly heavy stones with a length of black pipe; hammer one end to a chisel point.

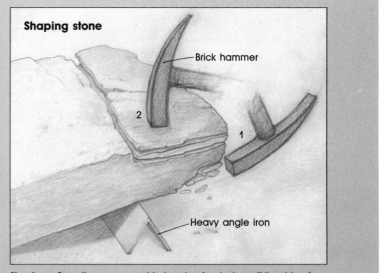

Shaping stone

Brick hammer

2

1

Heavy angle iron

Shaping—Sometimes you need to knock a few inches off the side of a stone to make it fit. Place it with the intended line of the break resting on the edge of another rock or a piece of heavy angle iron, as shown in the drawing. Chip away the bottom layers of stone (1). They'll fracture back to the point of contact with the support. Then knock away the top (2) to give you a flat face along the line you want.

Sylvester takes some care to overlap fill stones, and he rakes in pea gravel between layers of fill stones to fill gaps in the wall.

The finished wall is tight-fitting and handsome. Making a virtue of necessity, Sylvester made effective use here of several turtle-backed and wedge-shaped stones.

ble—shim them up if necessary, piecing underneath with rubble so they're solid.

As I go along, I shovel pea gravel into the fill to fill up gaps. I also like to have 3 in. or so of pea gravel between the fill and the bank, to improve drainage there.

I want the faces of my walls to be tight-fitting, with nice even courses. Every so often, I'll stand back and eyeball the face, then knock in protruding stones with a 3-lb. sledge or pry out receding stones with a small pry bar. If a face stone slants down at an awkward angle, I'll pry it up

and shim it back in line. When the wall looks good, I go back and fill gaps between the face stones with bits of rubble (a process called chinking). Any place you see a shadow or a dark spot, chink it in.

As the wall nears full height, the fill angles down from the face to the bank, and is topped by a wedge of soil. If you're planting lawn, you don't need much soil. If you're planting a garden or making a planter, the soil can be deeper immediately behind the caps, but use good-size cap stones. I mortar the caps in place, but

I keep the mortar well back so it doesn't show on the face. On top, you can fill gaps between cap stones with mortar or soil.

Fitting together a stone wall is a little like putting together a jigsaw puzzle. The pieces are heavier, but you still need to use your head to figure out where they go. If you take your time and get them to fit, you'll have fun and your wall will last a long time. ☐

Jim Sylvester does a variety of stonework in Williamstown, Massachusetts.

Splitting—If a load of stone is short on good cap, face or tie stones, you can sometimes split the ones you've got to increase your stock. The stone must be evenly layered, like mica schist. The layers, or "grain," appear as differences in color along its edges—a band of gray gives way to red, or dark gray to lighter. The grain of other types of layered stone is often as easy to make out.

To split a stone, prop it up and drive a 3-in.-wide cold chisel between two layers with a 3-lb. sledge, as shown in the photos above. A large stone may require a couple of chisels. Start both and work them down together, so you don't pop a corner off. I've gotten as many as half a dozen identical cap stones out of a perfectly layered stone 12 in. to 15 in. thick. —J.S.

A bamboo fence serves as an attractive addition to almost any garden. Simple designs, like this *yotsume-gaki,* or "four-eyed fence," are easy to make.

Fencing With Bamboo
How to make a useful garden accent

by David Flanagan

amboo fences can screen unsightly structures or unwanted views, and serve as attractive backgrounds for special features such as plantings, fountains and pools. They can also define boundaries and provide privacy. Smaller bamboo constructions like gates or trellises add decorative accents to any garden.

The Chinese and Japanese have made an art form of bamboo fencing, but you needn't have a Chinese or Japanese garden to make good use of a bamboo fence. It is appropriate in most settings, and offers a pleasant change from what we in the West usually see.

Some fence designs require only whole poles (called culms). Others are made

David Flanagan, the Bamboo Fencer, lives in Jamaica Plain, Massachusetts.

A septum stretches across the interior of a culm at each node. Placing a septum at the top of a picket or post helps prevent rot. The saw cut visible in these culms relieves stresses and helps prevent unwanted cracks.

from slats, which are a cinch to make since bamboo splits true and easily. Some fences incorporate whole culms with slats woven into lattices or solid panels. In this article, I'll show you how to make a simple, open boundary fence of whole culms, shown in the photo above and the drawings. Using the same technique for wiring and tying the pieces together, you can make a variety of other bamboo designs.

Bamboo background

First, you need to know a little about the structure of bamboo. Bamboo is a woody grass, and culms are the hollow, upright stems. The prominent lines around a culm are called nodes; leaves and branches originate there. Inside the culm at each node is a diaphragmlike disk called a septum. Most bamboos are hollow between septums.

Bamboo is durable. Its hard, smooth skin needs no protective paint. Different bamboos have characteristic skin textures (though the most exotic forms are too expensive to use for fencing). Exposed to

Photos: top, Staff; bottom, Greg Cranna

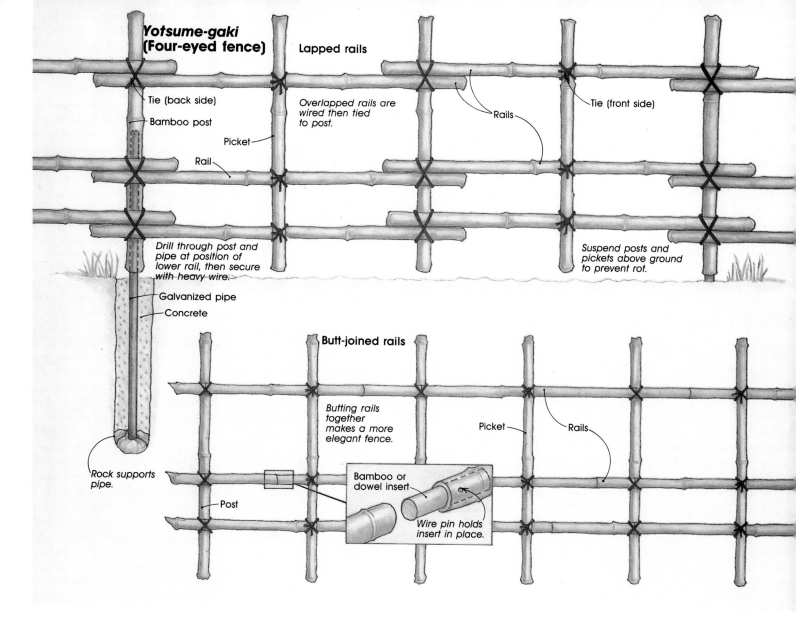

Yotsume-gaki (Four-eyed fence)

Lapped rails

Tie (back side)

Bamboo post

Picket

Overlapped rails are wired then tied to post.

Rails

Tie (front side)

Rail

Drill through post and pipe at position of lower rail, then secure with heavy wire.

Suspend posts and pickets above ground to prevent rot.

Galvanized pipe

Concrete

Butt-joined rails

Butting rails together makes a more elegant fence.

Picket

Rails

Rock supports pipe.

Post

Bamboo or dowel insert

Wire pin holds insert in place.

---

sun and weather, the skin of all bamboos eventually loses its natural oils and turns a pleasant, weathered gray. If you prefer, weathering can be retarded with wax—liquid floor polish is easy to apply, and an application two or three times a year can hold off weathering for five to six years.

The only insect that's likely to infest bamboo fencing is the powder-post beetle, and this is a problem only in humid locations with mild winter temperatures. Most imported bamboos are fumigated to kill any beetles or larvae present when they enter the country.

Fence basics

Making a bamboo fence is not quite as simple as it might seem when you look at a photograph of the finished thing. It's the "devil in the detail" that's missing in photos: Is that a whole piece of bamboo or is it split? How are those two round, slick pieces attached? Do those rope ties really hold it all together?

Fasteners—Beneath the good-looking ties that show in photographs are the wires that actually hold the fence together. The ties add some strength to the joint, but they're not enough. Interestingly, Americans have a harder time accepting the wires' presence than the Japanese do. My clients insist that I hide the wires, but in Japan no one bothers. I use heavy-duty galvanized wire (called galvanized temporary tie wire) to assemble large bamboo fences, which can be quite heavy. For lighter work, like the trellis shown on p. 32, a copper wire of about 15 gauge is traditional. Such wire is normally available at hardware stores, where it's sometimes sold as 0.050-in. wire.

The Japanese use a lot of ties in their fences, and these are very decorative. The traditional material is a two-strand twine made from the fibers of palm trees. It's about ¼ in. thick and comes in cocoa brown and black. Black is most commonly used on boundary and decorative fences, the cocoa brown in less prominent locations. The black fades in the sun, and the dye runs when wet. It will be visibly gray in a year. Palm twine is very rot-re-sistant, coarse, and hard on the hands to tie. But the knot holds as if it were welded.

An alternative to natural-fiber twine is ⅜-in. three-strand black polypropylene line. This material is very tough, will not fade in the sun and is completely water-resistant. But it's slippery. I cut the line with a soldering tool and fuse the knots with an electric paint stripper.

Posts—Like most woody material, bamboo rots if kept wet. To prolong a fence's life, use rot-resistant cedar or pressure-treated posts, or slip the bamboo over galvanized steel pipe embedded in concrete. The bamboo's convenient hollow center makes this easy. If you want to set bamboo posts in the ground, pack alternating layers of gravel and soil in the hole around them. The improved drainage will add several more years to the life of the posts.

Tools—You don't need special tools for working bamboo. A hacksaw, radial-arm saw or tablesaw works just fine for cutting culms to length. Bamboo has an unusually high silica content, which makes the culm hard and provides insect and rot resistance. It also dulls saw blades rapidly. If you're going to cut much bamboo, carbide-tipped saw blades are well worth the extra cost. To bore holes, regular twist drills work fine. You'll need standard wire cutters, or electrician's side-cutters, for cutting wire and palm twine.

Making a fence

The *yotsume-gaki,* or "four-eyed fence," is probably the most used and easily constructed of the Japanese bamboo fences. It is an open fence that delineates boundaries between different garden areas or activities. Fences of this type range in height from 2 ft. to 6 ft., and are made of culms from ¾ in. to 4 in. in diameter. The three-tier version shown here is the most popular.

After completing the mandatory first three steps of a fencing job—measure, re-measure, and finally measure it again—make a scale drawing of a panel (the span between posts). Once you're satisfied with the design, you can figure out and order the material you'll need (see Resources on the facing page). To allow for waste, add 6 in. for each piece requiring a node at the end.

The length of a panel depends on what looks good to you, on the weight the rails must support and on the length of the culms available for rails. For this fence, I decided to make all the rails, posts and pickets of 2-in.-dia. Tonkin bamboo, but they could be different diameters from one another. I don't make panels with 2-in. Tonkin longer than 10 ft. The higher the pickets, the shorter I make the panels.

The posts and pickets are equally spaced, but equally spaced rails are boring. I play with their spacing until I find one that's interesting but not jarring. You can overlap the rails at the posts, or butt them, which gives a more formal look. To butt-join the rails, you'll have to insert a dowel of the appropriate diameter into the ends of the culm, as shown in the drawing on p. 29. Wooden posts are usually placed between two regularly spaced pickets on the back, or least-viewed, side of the fence. If they're darker than the bamboo, the wooden posts almost seem to disappear.

Begin construction by cutting all the pieces to length. I cut the posts and pickets so each will have a node with an intact septum on top. This wastes some material, but it excludes water and helps prevent stains and rotting. It doesn't matter where the nodes fall on the rails, though I like the rails to show a node and septum at the ends of the fence and at gate openings. If your saw is coarse, wrap the area to be cut tightly with masking tape beforehand to reduce fraying. Take the sharp edge off

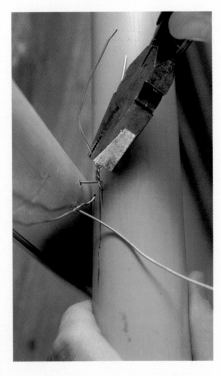

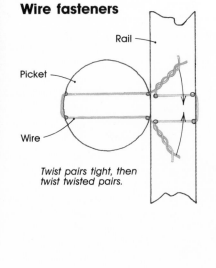

Wire is what really holds the bamboo poles together. Drill two holes side by side in each piece, thread the wire through and twist the pairs together as shown at left. Then twist the twisted pairs together, trim the ends and bend the remaining wire out of sight between the pieces.

Wire fasteners

Rail

Picket

Wire

Twist pairs tight, then twist twisted pairs.

the cut with light sanding.

Bamboo, like most woody materials, is subject to splitting when it alternately absorbs and loses water. These splits can be explosive. It's not at all uncommon for a 3-in.-dia. culm suddenly to split over a length of 12 ft. or so. It sounds like a pistol shot. Chemical treatments and banding are used to combat splitting, but I don't think these are worth the effort for fencing. If you want to control splitting, you can make a relief cut through each culm wall. This will allow the culm to expand and contract without building up large stresses.

I make a relief cut in all the pickets, posts and rails. The safe way to do this is with a router table. Use a ¼-in. straight bit, and set it high enough to cut through the culm wall. Make the cut along the entire length of the culm. Take special care to hold the culm firmly when making this and other cuts with power tools. Bamboo, being round and smooth, tends to roll, cock and bind the bit. Don't use a tablesaw to make this cut. The culm could roll, jam in the blade, and kick back with great force and velocity, causing serious injury.

Next, decide how to orient the pickets

To assemble a panel, author Flanagan lays out the rails and attaches pickets at each end, then works his way along, wiring pickets in place.

RESOURCES

Designing bamboo fences
A bamboo fence can be sculpture, eliciting an emotional response in almost anyone. The books listed below provide a wealth of fence ideas. Make sure to find out what your local building codes say about fences, too.

Bamboo Fences of Japan by Osamu Suzuki and Isamu Yoshikawa. Books Nippon, 1123 Dominguez St., Unit K, Carson, CA 90746. $36.95. Many beautiful photos.

The Book of Bamboo by David Farrelly. Sierra Club Books, c/o J.V. West, P.O. Box 11950, Reno, NV 89510. $25.00 hardcover, $14.95 paperback, plus $4.50 shipping. Covers many aspects of bamboo.

A Japanese Touch for Your Garden by Kiyoshi Seike et al. Kodansha International, 114 Fifth Ave., New York, NY 10011. $24.95. Good photos and garden-design guidance.

Buying bamboo
Bamboo is sold by the foot or the pole. The price increases with the diameter. Bought by the bundle, ½-in. poles 4 ft. long can cost as little as 20¢ each, while 10-ft. lengths of 6-in.-dia. bamboo can run $30 each. Unfortunately, shipping is a substantial part of the cost of timber bamboo. Some suppliers discount culms with splits in them. If your design allows you to place these splits where they're not objectionable, or if you're splitting your own strips, you can save money by buying these defective culms. The author recommends the following firms that sell fencing bamboo; several can help you choose an appropriate type and size.

Bamboo and Rattan Works Inc., 470 Oberlin Ave. South, Lakewood, NJ 08701-6997. 201-370-0220.

Bamboo Brokerage, 13245 Woodinville Redmond Rd., Redmond, WA 98042. 206-868-5166.

The Bamboo Company, 12981 SW 267th St., Homestead, FL 33032. 305-258-5868.

Bamboo Fencer, 31 Germania St., Bldg. D, Jamaica Plain, MA 02130. 617-524-6137.

Eastern Star Trading Company, 624 Davis St., Evanston, IL 60201. 800-522-0085.

Orion Trading Company, 820 Coventry Rd., Kensington, CA 94707. 415-540-7136.

and posts so the relief cuts will be least obtrusive. Fences viewed primarily from one side are easy—the cuts go on the back side. Two-sided fences are more problematic. Whatever you decide, be consistent. If the cuts are all oriented in the same direction or in a pattern, they can become an attractive part of the design. Relief cuts in rails and other horizontal members should always face down, so they won't collect water.

Mark the location of the rails on all the pickets and posts, then bore the holes for the wire fasteners. The Japanese often pass a single wire through a hole in both pieces and secure it with several twists around each piece. My clients don't like to see the wire, so I use the method shown in the photo and drawing at the top of the facing page, which allows me to hide the wire between the pieces. Bore the holes side by side across the width of the culm, but offset them slightly. The wire can pull through the wall of the culm if the holes are in line with each other. Make the holes about four times the diameter of the wire so it will be easy to thread through them. I use a ⅛-in. bit for 15-ga. copper wire. For the posts and the pickets adjacent to them, drill holes at the locations of all three rails. For the remaining pickets, drill for the top and bottom rails only. Ties are sufficient to hold the center rail in place on them. Mark and bore holes at the corresponding locations on the rails.

Next, cut and insert a wire in each pair of holes. The wires in the pickets and rails should extend about 2 in.; those in the posts should extend at least 6 in. because they have to go around the rails rather than through them.

I assemble the pickets and rails of all the panels in the shop, then attach them to the posts on site. To assemble a panel, I lay the three rails on a low table (a garage floor will do, too) and attach the first picket at each end, then work my way down the panel. To attach a picket to a rail, I pair the wire ends and twist them together, then twist the two resulting ends together again. I cut off excess wire and push the twisted mass into the intersection, out of sight.

I anchor the bamboo posts on galvanized pipe, as shown in the drawing on p. 29. The pipe should be a snug but not tight fit; 1⅜-in. o.d. pipe works well for 2-in. bamboo. For short fences, the pipe extends at least two thirds of the way up the post; for taller fences, I push it past at least two nodes. Clear septums and other obstructions from the bamboo with the sharpened end of a piece of pipe. (A blunt end will do; it's just more work.) I usually set the pipe in 3-ft.-deep holes; in cold climates, make sure the holes go deeper than the frost line.

I assemble the posts and pipes in the workshop, before installation. To hold them in place, bore a hole through both in line with the lowest rail, insert a piece of heavy galvanized wire and bend the ends down. The lower rail and its tie will cover the wire. The pipe will obstruct at least some of the holes for the wire that holds the rails, so drill through the pipe at this time to clear the way.

When you install the posts, be very careful to set them the correct distance apart, and stringline them at the proper height. Set the posts loose in the holes and secure the panel rails to them, then pour the concrete. The Ortho book *How to Design and Build Fences and Gates* (available at many hardware stores and garden centers) gives excellent instructions for setting posts, as well as other basics of fence-making.

There are many traditional designs for bamboo fences. But your imagination may well be where the best designs come from. Once the material is understood, and the fastening system mastered, you're ready to do your own thing and it could well be marvelous. Good luck. □

(For ideas for using bamboo, see next page.)

You can overlap the rails of adjacent panels and wire them to a post. You don't need to bore holes in the post for the wire that holds the upper rail.

Ideas for using bamboo

Bamboo is a versatile material for building garden gates, fences and ornaments. Using different sizes of poles and varying their spacing gives many styles and effects. Widely spaced medium-size poles can make a see-through gate and fence (above left) or a lightweight geometric trellis (below right). Closely fitted smaller poles and stems can lie smooth as corduroy (below left) or flare like a grass skirt (above right).

Photos: top left and top of facing page, Greg Cranna; all others, David Flanagan

A bamboo feature catches your attention in the winter, when the rest of a garden is buried under snow (above and below right). In better weather, bamboo's natural color, texture and form make a pleasing but unobtrusive background for a variety of other plants (below left).

An occasional waxing helps protect the surface of bamboo outdoors and keeps it from flaking and graying.

Layers of red and brown soil drift like clouds across a curving garden wall of rammed earth. Soot-blackened plaster and ceramic tiles cap the wall to fend off rain. Dividing a Japanese garden from a Western-style garden, the wall in its simplicity suits both.

All photos, except where noted: Hidefumi Morimiya

A Timeless Garden Wall
Rammed earth unites old and new gardens

by Marc Peter Keane

Can a garden wall look completely traditional yet modern too? My clients, father and son, had built a new house in Japan (the tradition that parents live with their eldest son is still observed in Japan today). To maintain privacy, they had split the house down the middle, and they intended to divide the garden as well. The son requested that his side be designed in a Western fashion while his parents wanted their side to be purely Japanese. Between the halves of the garden, I would have to build a suitable wall.

Rammed earth was the perfect solution. Plastered earth walls are used in traditional Japanese gardens, and the clean lines of a rammed earth wall look modern enough for a Western garden. To make the wall look even more contemporary—and to make it stronger—I decided to give it a serpentine shape. I hoped the wall would not just divide the two gardens but would link them as well.

Rammed earth
Making a rammed-earth wall is simple but exacting. You build a wooden form—basically a wall-sized box with no bottom or top—and fill it with a mixture of clay, sand and binders. You add a few inches of the mixture at a time and tamp each layer vigorously with a flat-faced ram. When you've filled the form to the top, you remove it to reveal the rammed earth. I'll tell you enough about building the garden wall so you can decide if you'd like to try rammed-earth construction. For more details, you should find a good book. [See *Adobe and Rammed Earth Buildings* by Paul Graham McHenry, Jr., University of Arizona Press.]

Rammed-earth walls have always impressed me as being "honest"—they reflect how honestly you have performed your work. In the construction of the forms, in mixing the soil and the binders, and especially in the ramming, there can be no mistakes or they will show in the wall. I can imagine rammed-earth construction as training for Zen monks—slow, repetitive hard work that must be done exactingly.

I drew on both Western and Japanese techniques for building the wall. To help the garden wall resist earthquakes, which are common in Japan, I made a foundation of reinforced concrete and brick. The founda-

tion also keeps the wall off the ground. Rammed-earth walls don't like wet feet—constant moisture weakens them. I made a shallow trough down the middle of the foundation so the earth wall is locked in place. I did not use anchor bolts or reinforcing in the wall because bolts eventually fracture the rammed earth.

Forms, dirt and rams
Forms for a rammed-earth wall must be strong because ramming creates enormous pressure and opposite sides cannot be joined together with ties that traverse the wall (the ties would make ramming impossible). My crew and I made the walls with layers of ¼ in. plywood and a curving wood frame. We fastened the walls together with ties running through the brick foundation below grade and between the tops of the posts 2 ft. above the finished height of the wall. From end to end, there were five form panels on each side. The impression of their joints divides the finished wall into five segments like a folding screen.

Rammed earth is weak at corners and durable on faces. To finish the ends of the wall without corners, we sawed a large plastic pipe in half lengthwise and fixed

The author and a helper stand atop curving wood forms to tamp the earth inside with rams made of square timbers. Ramming solidifies the nearly dry mix of clay, sand and binders (visible in both buckets) so the wall will stand alone and resist the elements when the forms are removed.

From the terrace of the Western-style garden, the serpentine shape, subtle colors and brick foundation of the rammed-earth wall look distinctively modern. To reinforce the effect, the author repeated the brick of the foundation along the perimeter of the terrace and patio.

the halves, standing upright, inside the ends of the forms. The pipe sections gave us smooth end curves but added small corners to the earth wall, which we took great care to ram properly.

For this garden wall, my clients and I wanted a "mountain and cloud" pattern—layers of different colors that rise and fall like gentle mountains and low clouds. Most rammed-earth walls are made of subsoil that is mined on the construction site to reduce costs. Because this garden site was small and urban, it had no soil to spare, so I went looking outside the city. For aesthetic reasons, we chose red and brown soils and had two loads delivered.

For strength, rammed-earth walls need the right proportions of clay, sand and binders. We adjusted our soils with reddish sand to get a mix of 70% sand and 30% clay. To bind the mix, we added some baked lime and white portland cement (regular gray cement kills

the color of the soil), along with a little nigari, a potassium salt that is used in Japanese rammed-earth floors (and to make tofu). The lime and cement make up about 10% of the mix by volume, and my crew mixed in the nigari by taste—literally.

We rammed the wall by hand. We could have used pneumatic tampers (to the delight of our backs), but I felt that hand ramming allowed for greater control. If you build only a garden wall, you won't need a pneumatic tamper (nor can you justify the expense) and, trust me, you will be filled with an immense satisfaction when the wall is complete...even if you can't move your arms for several days.

Here are a few hints for ramming. Coat the forms with a lubricant (we used creosote) so the earth won't stick to them. Ram thoroughly—there is no touching up later. When the sound of the ram changes to a dull thud that resonates throughout the form, you have tamped

Low-sheared azaleas dotted with pink flowers hug the beds, path and rocky pool of the Japanese garden. The rammed earth wall in the distance provides a traditional-looking backdrop and effectively screens the Western-style garden beyond.

enough. Don't add more than 6 in. of soil at a time. If you do, you'll compact the top but not the bottom. We worked with 2-in. to 4-in. layers. Take care with the sides and corners. Finally, if you ram part of a wall one day, the rammed earth may shrink slightly overnight and the next day's work will bulge over it. Either make your rule "one form, one day," or tighten the forms when you start work the next day.

The finishing touch

Rammed-earth walls need a roof. If rain seeps into the wall, freezing and thawing can rapidly break it apart.

We capped the garden wall with a layer of mortar, a layer of shikkui (lime plaster reinforced with fine fibers and blackened with soot) and a ridge of traditional tiles held down with thick copper wires set into the mortar below. We also spread a thin border of shikkui at the base of the wall, both for decoration and to protect the base from water damage. As a substitute for shikkui, white portland cement mixed with chopped fiberglass would work. It could be colored with an additive.

Though rammed-earth walls are commonly protected by wide caps, we made the cap narrow. The wall will dampen and grow darker with rain, then dry out and return to its original color, a barometer of the changes of weather.

Keeping the cap small will almost certainly speed up the weathering of the wall, but I don't mind. I even added slightly different amounts of binder to the different soils so that alternate layers will erode at different rates. I welcome the prospect. Among the most poetic scenes I have seen in Japan are the old earthen walls of Kyoto half eaten by time.   □.

Marc Peter Keane is a landscape architect from New York who lives and works in Kyoto, Japan.

Building a Picket Fence

Homemade pickets and decorative posts make a handsome fence

Lending a note of formality and precision, a homemade picket fence sets off the author's side yard and new flower beds.

by John M. Kenny

Inspired by a visit to Colonial Williamsburg, where many houses are complemented by attractive picket fences, my wife and I agreed that a picket fence would set off our side yard and the flower beds I planned to make there. The land slopes, and we liked the idea of a crisp linear fence crossing the yard in steps. We also hoped that the fence would add value to our home, accent the property, and keep our dog in his yard.

I designed the fence myself, with an arching gate and decorative tops on the pickets and fenceposts. You can readily modify the design to suit your tastes and skill at carpentry. If your imagination needs a start, you'll find a sampler of picket fences on p. 42.

Cutting posts, pickets and rails

I chose to make the fence entirely of pressure-treated lumber. Pressure-treated costs more than untreated lumber, but will last far longer, especially for posts. The pressure-treated lumber sold by most lumberyards is protected from decay and insects by compounds of chromium, copper and arsenic (the most common mix is abbreviated CCA) that bind chemically to the wood and give it a greenish tinge. A retention number indicates how much wood preservative the lumber holds. Lumber that contacts the ground or is likely to stay wet (fenceposts, for example) should be 0.40 retention. For other uses (pickets, for instance), the lumber can be 0.25 retention.

Handle pressure-treated lumber safely. The EPA rates the hazards as slight, but CCA wood preservatives are nonetheless toxic. Lumber sometimes emerges from treatment with a dusting of preservatives, which can be absorbed through the skin, so wear gloves. Avoid inhaling the sawdust by wearing a dust mask when you saw and sweep up. Do not burn the sawdust and wood scraps. Send them to your municipal landfill.

When you buy lumber, dig through the stacks at the lumberyard and select the straightest, least-knotty pieces. Knots can weaken lumber and bleed through paint.

Besides, the charm of picket fences depends on regularity and precision.

The fenceposts are 8-ft.-long 4x4s. The decorative tops, called finials, are my own design. I cut the spike with a bow saw, and the 1-in.-wide groove below it with a circular saw set at a 45° angle.

Making pickets takes a lot of repetitive work. My pickets are roughly 2⅝ in. wide, with curving tops and a notch on both sides. To make them, I first crosscut 8-ft.-long 1x6s in half, and then ripped the 4-ft.-long pieces down the middle. To shape the tops, I used a router and followed a template cut from particle board. Routing produced smooth, nearly identical pickets, but it was also slow, noisy and dusty. If I were to make more pickets, I'd cut the tops four at a time on a bandsaw. I'm sure I could crank out serviceable pickets at twice the pace, with half the sawdust. If you have only a circular saw, choose a picket design based on straight cuts.

I primed and painted all the posts, rails and pickets with white exterior acrylic paint before assembling the fence. Painting first is much quicker than painting a fence in place, and you can do a complete job, leaving no holidays.

Setting posts
Postholes have to be dug with reasonable precision. A hole out of line makes more work: you have to enlarge it so you can move the post to the right place, and if you're setting a post in concrete, you'll need more concrete to fill the hole.

For efficient digging, you need special tools. Most rental stores have both hand and power diggers. The gas-powered digger is basically an engine with handles and a 3-ft. to 4-ft. steel auger. I didn't try it, because I wasn't sure I could guide it accurately, even with help from a strong friend (those machines have a lot of torque). Being the cautious novice, I dug the holes by hand with a clamshell posthole digger, which has two opposed trowel-shaped blades and two 5-ft.-long wooden handles to open and close the blades. If your soil is rocky, you may have to invest in a digging bar, a solid-steel tool about 5 ft. long with a pointed or tapered end. When you hit a rock that your auger or clamshell digger can't move, you peck away the dirt around it, drive the point of the digging bar alongside it, and pry it loose.

Fenceposts have to be well anchored. Even with spaces between the pickets, a fence catches the wind. Pushed hard in storms year after year, fenceposts can loosen and start to lean. To make them solid, dig deep holes—30 in. to 36 in. deep—and pack soil firmly around the posts. If your soil is light, sandy or loose, or if the posts must bear extra strain, you may have to set them in concrete. By

adding thickness underground, concrete makes the posts harder to budge. I set only the gateposts and corner posts in concrete. I dug the holes 12 in. in diameter and about 3 ft. deep, and found that each hole needed almost one 60-lb. sack of premixed concrete. For the rest of the posts, I dug holes roughly 8 in. in diameter and 3 ft. deep, and refilled each with soil in 6-in. layers, tamping each layer thoroughly with a 2x4. I mounded the backfill around each post to prevent water from collecting.

Each post must stand perfectly upright and be the right height. The posts stand the same height above the pickets, except where the slope of the land obliges you to step the fence up or down, as shown in the photo below. Stretch a string

Picket fences cross sloping land in steps. Here, as the ground rises near the bottom of one fence section, the next section moves up 6 in.

between two stakes to mark the line of posts before you set them in place, and use a level to keep the posts plumb as you tamp the soil around them.

Assembling the fence and gate
I used metal brackets to connect the rails to the posts, as shown in the drawing on pp. 40-41. Made of galvanized steel with nail holes for fastening, these brackets are called rail holders. Mine cost 24¢ apiece at the lumberyard. You nail the rail holder to the post, then drop the 2x4 rail into the holder and nail it in place. Use galvanized nails, or rust will leave ugly brown stains on your white fence. The rail holders let me remove fence sections easily. I just pull two nails at each holder and the fence section lifts up and out.

Plumbing a post with plywood wedges

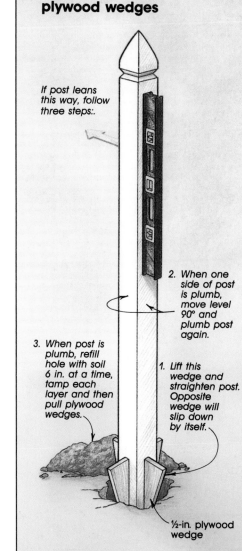

If post leans this way, follow three steps:.

2. When one side of post is plumb, move level 90° and plumb post again.

3. When post is plumb, refill hole with soil 6 in. at a time, tamp each layer and then pull plywood wedges.

1. Lift this wedge and straighten post. Opposite wedge will slip down by itself.

½-in. plywood wedge

Setting fenceposts plumb

by Bob Calvert
I've come up with a neat trick to simplify the job of setting fenceposts plumb (that is, perfectly upright). I borrow a helping hand from four plywood wedges. Here's how they work.

Set each post roughly upright by eye, at the right distance from its neighbor, and drop the wedges alongside it at 90° to each other. Now hold a hand level against the post in line with one of the wedges. Whichever way the post leans, lift the wedge slightly on the opposite side and tip the post toward it. The wedge on the side toward which the post was leaning will slip lower by itself. Then move the hand level around the post 90° and repeat the same steps. Your post is now plumb in all directions and firmly held by the wedges. Backfill the hole with dirt, tamping between the wedges, until the hole is three-quarters full. Then remove the wedges and finish backfilling and tamping, and the job is done. □

Bob Calvert lives in San Jose, California.

With the rails in place, I turned to the pickets. First I stretched a line from post to post to mark their tops. I nailed the first picket either in the center of the rail or offset half the width of a picket, depending on which would space the pickets evenly between the posts. Then I nailed on the rest of the pickets with 6d galvanized nails, using a spare picket for a spacer and checking with a level from time to time to make sure the pickets were plumb. I loosely nailed on pickets that covered rail hangers, so I could remove fence sections.

Constructing the gate was more complex. Mine is 4 ft. wide so I can push a wheelbarrow through without scraping my knuckles, and it has a fan shape made by pickets of different lengths. To endure the daily wear and tear, the 2x4 frame is made with half-lap joints, as the drawing below shows. I glued and screwed the half-laps with full-cure epoxy and stainless-steel screws. I gave the

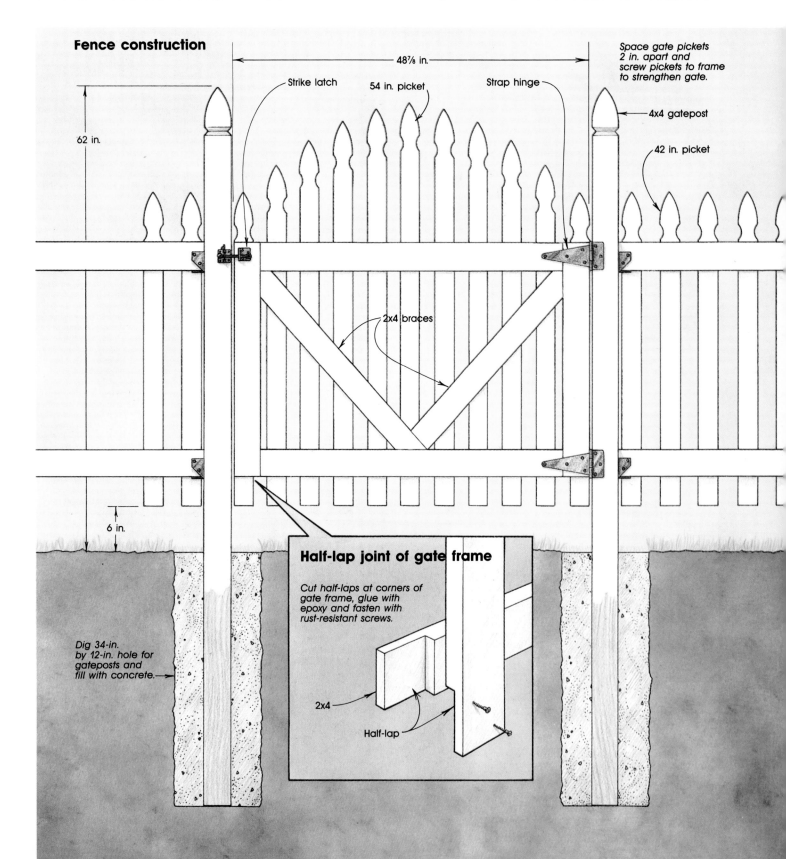

Fence construction

48⅞ in.

Strike latch   54 in. picket   Strap hinge

Space gate pickets 2 in. apart and screw pickets to frame to strengthen gate.

62 in.

4x4 gatepost

42 in. picket

2x4 braces

6 in.

Half-lap joint of gate frame

Cut half-laps at corners of gate frame, glue with epoxy and fasten with rust-resistant screws.

Dig 34-in. by 12-in. hole for gateposts and fill with concrete.

2x4

Half-lap

gate double 2x4 braces for symmetry, and screwed the pickets to the gate for more strength.

I hung the gate on galvanized-steel strap hinges, screwing the hinges to the gatepost and then to the gate, leaving a ¼-in. gap between gate and post. Check the fit carefully before you screw the gate in place. Level the gate, check the gap, and, if necessary, shave the edge of the gate with a hand plane to even it up. My gate has a simple galvanized-steel strike latch. I thought about something fancier, but ran out of time and desire.

The fence is a near-total success. I built it for half the cost of having a fence built, and it looks as good as we hoped it would. The only drawback is the 6-in. gap under the gate, which I plan to narrow with a brick walk. Much to my embarrassment, our dog has learned to slither under the gate and make the great escape. □

John Kenny lives in Annandale, Virginia.

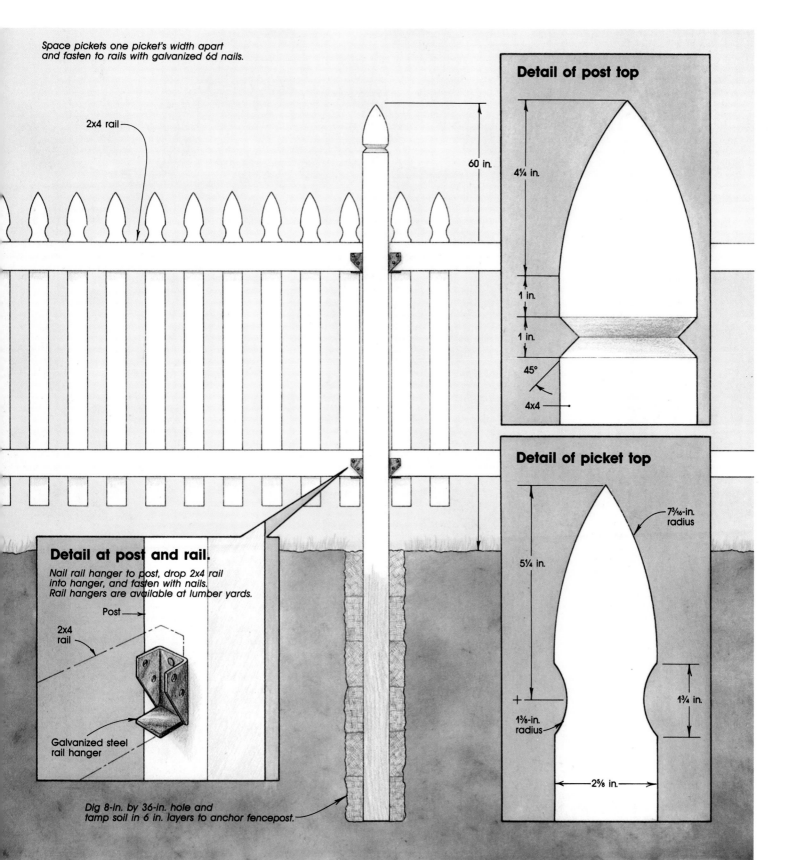

Space pickets one picket's width apart and fasten to rails with galvanized 6d nails.

2x4 rail

60 in.

Detail of post top

4¼ in.

1 in.

1 in.

45°

4x4

Detail of picket top

7⁹⁄₁₆-in. radius

5¼ in.

1³⁄₈-in. radius

1¾ in.

2⅝ in.

Detail at post and rail.
Nail rail hanger to post, drop 2x4 rail into hanger, and fasten with nails. Rail hangers are available at lumber yards.

Post

2x4 rail

Galvanized steel rail hanger

Dig 8-in. by 36-in. hole and tamp soil in 6 in. layers to anchor fencepost.

A sampler of picket fences

By varying the basic elements of a picket fence—the posts, rails and pickets—builders have created a wide range of fence designs, as the sampling on this page shows. All the fences are from Colonial Williamsburg, a recreation of the Virginia town as it might have looked in the 18th century. The distinctive wrought-iron hardware of the gates at Williamsburg—strap hinges, latches, and ball-and-chain gate closers—is available by mail-order. For drawings, dimensions, installation instructions and prices, write to Colonial Williamsburg Foundation, P.O. Box C, Greenhow Store, Williamsburg, VA 23187.

Five styles of picket fence from Colonial Williamsburg are sold mail-order by Walpole Woodworkers, under license to Colonial Williamsburg. For a brochure, write to Walpole Woodworkers, Inc., 767 East St., Walpole, MA 02081. —*Mark Kane*

Pickets of varying height produce an arching section of fence. Two saw cuts produce the bevel tops of the pickets, and the tapered finials of the posts are set off by two grooves.

Round-topped pickets and an arching gate produce an appealingly simple fence. The wrought-iron gate hardware consists of strap hinges hung on pintles (spikes with upright heads), and a substantial latch.

Exacting carpentry produces an elegant fence, with pyramidal-topped 1×1 pickets turned 45° and piercing the top rail.

Bandsawing or jigsawing permits many graceful picket designs, among them the onion-shaped tops shown here. The finial of the post echoes the picket tops.

Bevel-topped pickets in two heights make a distinctive, tiered fence. The wide spacing above leaves the garden open to view while the close spacing below keeps rabbits out.

The Art of Container Gardening

Beyond the simple pot of geraniums

A cascading container planting designed by the author helps to give a feeling of enclosure for a pool area. The composition builds upward from purple verbena to white petunias and blue salvia, capped off with a butterfly bush (*Buddleia* 'Pink Delight').

by Michael Bowell

hen I describe my plans for a container garden to a client, I find myself walking around the imaginary cluster of pots to show how they will fill the space, while indicating with my arms the topography created by plants of different heights. And with my hands I explain the shapes and textures that will soon give the spark of life to a deck or patio.

What need is there for such body language? If it's a simple pot of geraniums you want, there isn't any. But if you want something more, then you must think in terms of height, texture and shape, as well as color, when selecting your plants and containers. Many gardeners think of container gardens as static creations: pop in a few annuals, give them a little water, then stand back and wait for color. I think of container plantings as flower arrangements that change throughout the season.

All photos, except where noted: Staff

A group of containers is often more engaging than a lone pot. Here the author clusters several pots around a large pot in the background that holds the tall, pink-flowered mandevilla vine.

the eye away from something visually less appealing. Container plantings arranged around a sitting area or a Jacuzzi® can serve either as a backdrop or as a screen.

Once you've determined the container garden's role in the landscape, think about the architecture of the plantings. Consider height, width and depth to keep your living sculpture from fading into the two dimensional background. In my containers I use pieces of old bittersweet or grapevines, as flower arrangers do, to bring the eye up, out of the container, and then back down. Living vines can serve as either a vertical or a trailing element. In containers near walls I sometimes train more than one vine out of the pot at various angles on fishing line, creating cozy niches for patio chairs. I also like to fill containers with plants of varying heights and with plants that grow to different sizes over the course of the season. The arching stems of lilies, for example, pop out over lower-growing plants and explode with color.

Before choosing plants for a container garden, select the vessel itself. There are as many different possible containers as there are types of plants to put in them. In general, I try to match containers to their surroundings. In a formal setting, classical stone urns may be appropriate. In an informal setting—at a country house, for example—wood or terra cotta would be good choices.

An urn of petunias, New Guinea impatiens and begonias welcomes visitors with a harmonious mix of soft pinks.

I rarely use one container alone. One is not usually enough for a successful composition. I use two, three or more pots in clusters—larger containers toward the back and smaller ones in front. Placed this way, the plants go from ground level to eye level and beyond, creating vertical movement and a cascading effect. I also tuck small containers into large ones. For example, to perk up a flagging display, you can set a flowering orchid or a budding perennial lily, still in its pot, on top of the soil of a larger pot, instantly integrating it into the scheme of your arrangement. The leaves of the other plants camouflage the pot.

When you are ready to choose plants for your containers, keep contrast in mind. Contrast is the dynamism of the planting, creating a rhythmic flow for the eye to follow. A container isn't interesting if all you see is a blur. I always strive for strong contrast in the sizes of plants, their shapes and their leaf textures.

There will always be heated debates about which color combinations are successful and which aren't. In

My containers are not low maintenance. I aim for an attractive display from earliest spring to late fall, so I plant and transplant, pinch and train, all season long. I enjoy the control I have over these tiny gardens, control I don't have over any other part of my five-acre property. You may not have the time or the energy to exercise the same kind of control over your containers, but you can borrow some principles of design and choice of plants from my containers and improve the looks of your potted arrangements. (For the cultural techniques of gardening in a container, see "Container Basics" on p. 47.)

Assembling the pieces

Designing a container garden is a matter of arranging plants in a way that is both artistically pleasing and suited to the health of the plants. I start by visualizing the role that the planting will play. Container plantings can extend the ground level garden up steps or onto a patio as a transition from flowing plant forms to the hardness of concrete, wood or brick. Container plantings also can be used either to attract or to distract the viewer's eye. Two containers placed a short distance from one another can frame a view and, at the same time, direct

The warm colors of 'Mini Balcomb Coral' geranium, 'Peter Pan Flame' zinnia and yellow *Zinnia linearis*, complemented by blue *Salvia farinacea* 'Victoria', catch the eye from a distance.

traditional favorites. I experiment extensively with different varieties of all sorts of plants. I also go to trial gardens at universities or botanical gardens to see how new cultivars are faring in our area. In general, I look for plants that are tough in the face of thunder showers, heat waves and insect pests, that look good all season long and that bear flowers that show up well from a distance. I also look for unusual colors in flowers or foliage for the variety they add to a color scheme. I often use my own containers as a laboratory. If a new variety consistently out-performs an old one, I begin to use it in all my plantings.

You may have to hunt a little to find uncommon plants. Because of the volume of my business, I can have plants custom grown by local nurseries. But I also grow a number of out-of-the-ordinary plants from seed. I usually order seed of particular varieties in a single

the end, it's a matter of personal taste. Do whatever works for you, but remember that in a container garden, the colors are concentrated and viewed at close hand. The same combinations that blend harmoniously in a meadow can be visual cacophony in a planter box that sits a few feet from your front door. Aim for a mixture of softer colors for areas near where people sit. Use hotter colors in containers that are farther from view.

Choosing plants

Many gardeners limit their container plant palette to the same old annuals. Don't! Open your mind to the enormous range of plants that can thrive in containers. I'll use anything in a container. Bulbs, perennials, shrubs and even trees can do very well in large pots or tubs. Making use of such unexpected plants allows you to design incredibly varied and dynamic plantings.

Including bulbs, perennials and woody plants in a container garden does require some extra effort, though. In cold-winter climates such as we have here in south-eastern Pennsylvania (USDA Zone 6), many plants that are perfectly hardy in the ground will perish if left outdoors in a pot. These plants make for very expensive annuals; to ensure their survival for next year's container plantings, transplant them into the ground in the fall.

I put some unusual plants in my containers, but many of the plants I use are uncommon cultivars of

The Swan River daisy in the lower left corner is an exceptional container plant because of its sprawling habit and its season-long flower show. In this container, the author combines its small purple daisies and needle-like leaves with petunias and a trailing verbena.

color, but I also try mixes every year. I always find a color shade in the mix that isn't available as a single color variety.

A selection of favorites

To give a better idea of how I choose plants and combine them, I've picked out a few of my favorites. Some of these will be familiar to you; others will be new. If you can't find the exact plant I recommend, try another, similar one. The important thing is to experiment.

Swan River daisy

(*Brachycome iberidifolia*)—This prostrate, thread-leaved annual produces myriads of small, purple daisies in all but the hottest weather and carries on until hard frost. It looks great trailing over the side of a container where it makes a nice contrast to the bolder flowers of *Nierembergia* 'Purple Robe' or the feathery blue of ageratum. I buy it, as I do many annuals, in hanging baskets from a local garden center. These baskets appear to be more expensive than six-packs, but when you see the size of the six-odd plants you get when you pull the clump apart, you'll realize that you're getting a deal.

Honeysuckle fuchsia

(*Fuchsia* 'Gartenmeister Bohnstedt')—Unlike the trailing fuchsia you see in hanging pots, this one has an upright growth habit, reaching 18 in. to 24 in. tall. You can grow it alone as a specimen plant; its salmon-orange flowers go beautifully with its bronzy foliage. But the honeysuckle fuchsia also combines well with other plants. Try it with the similarly warm colors of a golden variegated ivy or coral multiflora petunias. For a cooler, tapestried effect, combine it with purple petunias. The honeysuckle fuchsia takes hot sun well, but will also tolerate shade. It flowers all season long, right up to cold weather. Like its namesake, the honeysuckle fuchsia also attracts hummingbirds.

Bleeding-heart

(*Dicentra spectabilis*)—The old-fashioned bleeding-heart (USDA Zone 2) makes a great early-to-

midseason container plant. It flowers prolifically for me from mid-April through early July. When it starts to fade, I cut it to the soil level and fill in around it with annuals. In the fall, I dig up the roots and overwinter them in the ground. In the spring, I lift them and put them back in a container. Combine bleeding-hearts with tulips, ranunculus, pansies and lobelia for an early-season container. Include some cold-tolerant mainstays of the summer garden, such as verbena, to fill in as the cool-season plants fade.

Butterfly bush

(*Buddleia davidii*)—There are a number of butterfly bush cultivars from which to choose. I particularly like 'Pink Delight'. The long-lasting pink flower spikes go nicely with *Verbena bonariensis*, a wonderfully tall "see-through" plant topped with clusters of lavender-mauve flowers. I use butterfly bush year after year in some of my larger containers where its 5-ft. to 6-ft. size provides adequate height and mass. I overwinter the plants, which are hardy to Zone 5, in the ground, pruning them back hard each spring to keep them in scale. If a butterfly bush gets too large, I either find a spot for it in the garden or I "bonsai" it—controlling its size by severely pruning both roots and top.

Mandevilla

—I recommend the cultivar 'Alice Dupont' for its 3-in. wide, pink trumpet flowers that stand out in a crowded planter. I train this fast-growing tropical vine up stakes, up a pole or up a wall. 'Alice Dupont' adds height to a pink container planting. Try it with *Verbena* 'Sissinghurst Pink' or an annual vinca (*Catharanthus*) such as 'Pretty 'n Pink'. It also looks good in a mass of vines, combining well with the smaller flowers of its neighbors. I love it with the purple-veined foliage, pink, sweet pea-like flowers and bright purple seed pods of the hyacinth bean (*Dolichos lablab*).

Contrasting shapes, textures and foliage colors enliven container plantings. The silvery, cut leaves of dusty miller (above) set off bolder green foliage and the flowers of bright pink geraniums, verbenas and pinks, deep purple petunias and magenta cockscomb.

Michael Bowell is the owner of Flora Design Associates, which specializes in indoor and outdoor garden design in West Chester, Pennsylvania.

Container Basics

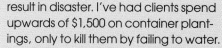

by Karen Kienholz Steeb

I do all sorts of landscape design, but container gardens are my specialty. I've planted and maintained hundreds of containers here in Washington State, and along the way I've learned what makes container plants thrive and what makes them falter. There are three basic steps to successful container gardening. First, provide your plants with a suitable growing environment—a large container and a well-drained growing medium. Second, plant closely within the container. And third, practice regular maintenance.

The primary purpose of a container is to serve as a receptacle for soil and plants. Although you want to select planters that are attractive, remember that they must also be functional. Choose containers of ample size. I recommend using containers that are at least 12 in. wide and 12 in. deep. Smaller containers require constant watering in warm weather. They're also more prone to freezing if left outside over winter, even in a relatively mild climate.

A container must also have good drainage. Without drainage, roots will be deprived of oxygen and will soon suffocate and rot. Most containers sold for planting have drainage holes in the bottom. If you choose a container that doesn't have holes, ask the store to drill some or do it yourself. Three to seven ½-in. holes are sufficient.

Once you have selected containers and set them in place, fill them with a soil mix. A container creates a demanding environment for plants. There is less insulation for the roots from temperature fluctuations, and the plants are closer together than they would normally be in the ground, so competition for nutrients and moisture is especially fierce. A lightweight soil helps plants adjust by giving them a good medium for root growth. I use one of the soilless mixes

available at any garden center. I avoid garden soil because it can carry weed seeds, insects and diseases.

Whatever plants you select for your container garden, I recommend that you plant much more closely than you would in the ground. Close planting makes the container look full immediately and increases the likelihood that the container will continue to look full as the plants grow. I don't have an easy rule of thumb for spacing. It depends on the

Close planting and a large container are keys to successful container gardening.

plant. For example, I space annuals purchased in a 4-in. nursery pot on 5-in. to 6-in. centers. I might transplant annual lobelia from a six-pack on 1½-in. to 2-in. centers. In general, I try to use enough plants to conceal the edges of the container and to all but hide the soil. I want the top of the container to be a vegetative tapestry from the moment I plant it.

Now that you've found just the right containers and filled them with a beautiful combination of plants, it's time to sit back and relax, right? Wrong. To get the most out of your containers, you must maintain them. The more attention you pay to watering, fertilizing and grooming, the better your container plantings will look. One thing is certain—neglect will

result in disaster. I've had clients spend upwards of $1,500 on container plantings, only to kill them by failing to water.

Watering is crucial to a planting's survival. Your climate, the size of your containers, the material they're made of and their location in your garden will determine how often your containers must be watered. I check mine every other day, every day in hot weather. Unless I can see the soil pulling away from the inside of the container (a clear sign of drought), I don't trust my eyes. I stick my finger into the soil. If the soil is dry 1 in. deep, I water. Avoid watering on a schedule; you will inevitably end up either under- or over-watering.

Most soilless mixes don't contain enough of the big three plant nutrients—nitrogen, phosphorus and potassium—to support plant growth for any length of time. And frequent waterings quickly wash out whatever nutrients are present. So it's important to provide a constant supply of fertilizer to plants in containers. At planting time, I sprinkle a slow-release fertilizer (analysis 14-14-14) onto the soil surface. For containers planted with annuals, I supplement the slow-release fertilizer every two weeks with an application of a water-soluble 20-20-20 formula. This may sound like overkill, but in my experience, container plants that receive this extra dose flower more prolifically than those that don't.

When I water, I take time to groom each container, removing spent blossoms and brown leaves. Continuous clean-up is very important, because containers usually sit in prominent locations and are viewed close up. Grooming also allows you to spot insect infestations and diseases before they spread.

Karen Kienholz Steeb is a landscape designer in Woodinville, Washington.

Handmade Stone

Making planters with cement, sand and peat moss

by Jan Kowalczewski Whitner

I first saw hypertufa on a visit to English gardens. There, collectors of alpine and rock plants use this mix of cement, sand and peat moss to make rectangular containers, traditionally 2 ft. to 4 ft. long and not quite as wide, with sharp edges and weathered surfaces. Set on stone pedestals or concrete blocks, these receptacles look like pocket Stonehenges, and their angular planes serve as perfect foils to the sturdy little rock plants living in them. The containers seem as ancient as the stone and rock that surround them, and they give a kind of time-worn distinction to the gardens they inhabit.

The development of hypertufa was prompted by English gardeners' fascination with plants that require special growing conditions. Alpine and rock plants need sharp drainage and like to nestle their roots next to rock surfaces, so it's a challenge to grow them outside their natural environment. In the early 1900s, English gardeners discovered a unique resource — old stone sinks from cottage kitchens and stone livestock troughs from the countryside — and converted these abandoned vessels into planting containers. These improvised planters proved ideal for alpine and rock plants, because the porous texture of sandstone, limestone

or tufa (a coarse-textured porous rock) draws moisture from soil evenly and consistently. But the supply of real stone sinks and troughs was quickly diminished, so enterprising gardeners developed hypertufa as an alternative. It duplicates the growing environment provided by natural stone containers, and also the colors and textures of real stone.

When I first saw hypertufa containers in England, their textures and shapes seemed so intriguing that the plants inside them held only minor interest for me. But once I returned home to Washington and made a few containers, the question of what to plant in them naturally came up. Knowing little about alpine and rock plants except their reputation for being difficult to grow, I decided to experiment with herbs, low-growing perennial flowers, mosses, succulents and bonsai instead. The results show that hypertufa containers display common and humble plants to their best advantage, just as they showcase rare and special ones.

The ingredients for hypertufa — cement, sand and peat moss — are readily available at local building or garden centers. For cement, buy portland cement. Avoid

Author Whitner uses hypertufa, a mix of cement, sand and peat moss, to make plant containers and garden ornaments that look as if they're carved from real stone. Shown growing above, clockwise from left, are candytuft, aubrieta, saxifrage and woolly thyme.

prepared cement mix that contains gravel, as it gives a coarse texture to the finished container. If you want to warm up the cold gray color of the cement, you can buy concrete colorants, powders in various shades of black, brown, yellow and green. A little colorant goes a long way — using more than a pinch per batch has left me with finished containers that almost glow in the dark.

For sand, I recommend fine-textured masons' sand, because it makes a stronger container than coarser grades of sand do. Instead of sand, you can use perlite or vermiculite — they're much lighter in weight, and give a nubby texture to the finished container. (To me, though, containers made with sand look more like natural stone.) I buy the third ingredient, peat moss, by the bale. Before using it, I pick out any unmilled chunks of peat or sticks of wood.

Making hypertufa containers is inexpensive. I usually pay a little over $3 a bag for 94-lb. bags of portland cement and 100-lb. bags of masons' sand, and about $10 for a 4-cu.-ft. bale of peat moss. One bag of cement, one bag of sand and 2 cu. ft. of peat moss is sufficient to make about ten hypertufa containers that each measure 12 in. by 13 in. by 5 in., with walls 1½ in. thick. (A container this size weighs 20 lb. to 22 lb.)

In addition to buying the ingredients, you'll need to assemble some common tools and equipment. I measure ingredients in an old 2-gal. bucket with quart quantities indicated inside, mix the components in a large, shallow plastic trough, and wear thick rubber gloves while I'm working. You should also have a short piece of ½-in. or thicker dowel, a steel chisel and a wire brush.

Finally, you'll need a mold that has the size and shape you require, and plastic garbage bags for lining the mold. For large containers—those wider or longer than 2 ft., for example, wooden molds are a good idea. For the smaller containers that I like to make, it's easier to use old metal or rubber dishpans, large pots or pans, plastic pots or tubs, or other containers I find at garage sales and second-hand stores.

I haven't reinforced any of the hundreds of small containers I've made over the last few years. I sell them at garden centers, besides using them in my own garden, and so far I haven't had any complaints of cracking or breakage—they've all survived moving and handling, and have weathered Seattle's mild winters. Reinforcing small containers with hardware cloth is relatively costly, time-consuming and, in my experience, counterproductive, because the cloth reinforcement sometimes prevents proper bonding at the corners. (See the sidebar on p. 51 for an easier method of reinforcing larger containers for a more severe climate.)

Making a container

I'll explain the process of making a rectangular trough. The same basic methods apply to containers of different sizes and shapes as well. I start by gathering my materials and equipment, and usually work in the basement, because it doesn't matter if I spill water on the floor there.

To make a trough with outside dimensions of 12 in. by 13 in. by 5 in., I use an old dishpan for an outer mold, lining it with a thin plastic garbage bag to keep the hypertufa from sticking to the mold as it dries. In addition, I sometimes use a small plastic dish or pan as an inner mold, to shape the opening inside the trough.

The texture of a finished hypertufa container depends upon the proportions of cement, sand and peat moss used to make it. I always measure these ingredients by volume, not by weight. For the trough described, I'd use about 3 qt. of portland cement, 3 qt. of sand and 6 qt. of peat moss (a 1:1:2 ratio) to get a tufalike texture. For a texture like sandstone, I'd increase the amount of sand to 4½ qt. and reduce the volume of peat moss to 4½ qt. (a 1:1½:1½ ratio). I mix the peat moss and sand together first, then add the cement and mix everything together by hand (wearing gloves, of course). This is the time to add a pinch of concrete colorant, if desired.

After combining the dry ingredients, I add water a little at a time, blending the

Step 1: To make a small hypertufa trough, Whitner measures about 3 qt. of cement, 3 qt. of sand and 6 qt. of peat moss into a mixing tray. She mixes the dry ingredients thoroughly by hand, then adds water a little at a time to bind the materials together.

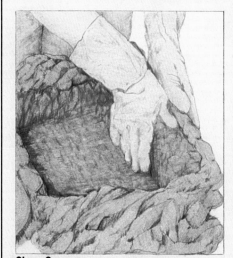

Step 2: Whitner packs the hypertufa mix into a plastic-lined mold, shaping the walls about 1½ in. thick. If the mixture is relatively dry, it will hold its shape without an inner mold.

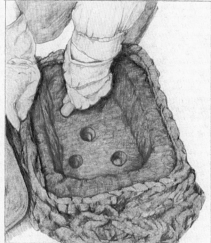

Step 3: After patting the hypertufa firmly into the mold to eliminate air pockets, Whitner uses a ½-in. dowel to carve out three or more drainage holes in the bottom.

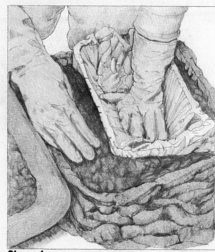

Step 4: If the mix is relatively moist, Whitner packs it between an inner and an outer mold. She covers newly molded containers with plastic, and lets them sit for 24 hours or longer.

Step 5: Once the mix has semi-hardened in a mold, Whitner scrapes the surface with a chisel and then brushes it to bring out the stone-like texture.

Illustrations: Laura B. Goodwin

mixture thoroughly after each addition. If the mixture is fairly dry, just wet enough to bind the materials together, the finished container will have a dense and relatively smooth surface. If the mix is wetter, with a consistency like cottage cheese, the surface texture will be more irregular. Either way, the results look nice.

I fill the bottom of the mold first, making a layer about 1½ in. thick and pressing the hypertufa mix down firmly to eliminate air holes or pockets. Then I use the dowel to carve out three or more ½-in.-dia. drainage holes. If I'm working with a dry mixture, I shape it by hand to the sides of the mold, building up walls about 1½ in. thick. If the mixture is wetter, I wrap the inner mold in plastic and set it on top of the mixture on the bottom of the outer mold, then I fill in the space between the two molds with the hypertufa mix.

After filling the mold, I fold the plastic over the top of the hypertufa to keep it from drying too fast, and leave it undisturbed for 24 hours or longer. I let the container sit until it's dry enough to be handled, but not so dry that it's hard to "weatherize" it—that is, to give it the texture and character of worn stone. I know it's ready when I can't dent the surface with my finger, but can still scratch it with a fingernail. Weatherizing the container is a satisfying step. First, I unmold the semihard container and remove any plastic sheeting that sticks to it. With a chisel or a gouge, I make a series of parallel marks along diagonal lines to mimic the tool marks in cut stone. Then I use a wire brush to roughen the surface of the hypertufa, and an old paintbrush to remove any clinging bits of sand or other debris.

When I'm satisfied with the surface, I set the container where it can "cure" for four to six weeks, protected from direct sunlight and temperatures below freezing. Freshly cured containers are still too alkaline from the chemicals released in the wetted cement to be suitable for growing plants. In order to neutralize the chemicals, I set cured containers outside and let the rain wash them for several weeks, or I wash them with the hose. You can use potassium permanganate crystals (available at industrial chemical-supply stores) to speed up the neutralization process. Mix the crystals with water to produce a Chianti-colored solution, brush it over the surface of the container, and wait several hours before washing it off. Dispose of the used solution away from animals and plants.

Planting

Growing plants in hypertufa containers looks more interesting, but isn't any more difficult, than growing them in other planters. I start with either good garden soil or purchased potting soil. For plants that need rapid drainage, I add equal

In addition to containers for plants, Whitner uses hypertufa to make garden ornaments such as stepping-stones and water basins.

measures of washed sand and perlite to the soil, place a ½-in. layer of gravel or stone on the bottom of the container before adding the amended potting soil, and raise the container off the ground on bricks or blocks to encourage faster draining after watering. For plants that need moister soil, I add peat moss and leaf mold to increase water retention, and spread a 1-in. layer of coarse peat moss in the bottom of the container before planting it. Sometimes I mulch the soil in planted containers with a layer of turkey grit (a kind of gravel that's sold at feed stores).

The first plants I tried in hypertufa containers were herbs. Their compact and grayish foliage looks good with the textures and shapes of the containers, and they appreciate the good drainage that hypertufa provides. Plants of woolly thyme (*Thymus lanuginosus*) and rupturewort (*Herniaria glabra*) liked their hypertufa environment so well that they crawled over the sides of the containers and down into the cracks between the bricks below them. These containers are sitting on the edge of a hot and sunny terrace near a patch of lavender, chives and sage, and their stony texture brings the effect of a rocky herb-covered Mediterranean hillside to one corner of our Pacific Northwest garden.

Next I planted some containers with flowering plants that have leaves similar in shape and texture to the low-growing herbs. One of my favorites is pink saxifrage (*Saxifraga rosacea*, the pink variety), a cushiony mound of short, fleshy leaves that's covered in spring by wiry flower stalks 6 in. high. The stalks support flowers of a bright, deep pink that really

sings against the gray hypertufa, and when the flowers fade, the fresh, light-green leaves still look handsome for the rest of the summer.

Many other plants with pink, red, white or lemon-yellow flowers look good in hypertufa. I like cheddar pink (*Dianthus gratianopolitanus*), thrift (*Armeria maritima*), moss campion (*Silene Schafta*), aubrieta (especially *Aubrieta deltoidea* 'Red Carpet'), candytuft (*Iberis sempervirens*) and stringy stonecrop (*Sedum lineare*). These plants surge over the sides of the containers as the growing season progresses, and they look especially nice positioned atop a low, wide wall. I place containers with plants in bloom so they can be seen from inside the house. When they've finished flowering, I move the plants back to a spot where their leaf form and texture complement the surrounding vegetation, and bring out other containers whose plants are beginning to bloom. This recurring movement of containers helps make the garden a dynamic landscape.

A Northwest garden nearly always has a cool, shady and moist corner in it. We plant hypertufa containers in such areas with mosses and selaginellas. Mosses love hypertufa and will grow on its surface naturally in rainy climates. In areas where mosses are not so invasive, you can encourage their growth on the containers by pouring buttermilk over the hypertufa and gently pressing small patches of moss onto it. Keep the surface moist and shaded until the moss is looking robust, and then place the container in a part of your garden that duplicates as closely as possible the original growing conditions of the moss. Another choice for dappled shade is Scotch moss (*Sagina subulata*; not a true moss). The cultivar 'Aurea' makes a lime-green mat sporting starry flowers, which is guaranteed to light up any spot it's placed in, however dark and dreary the area may be.

Succulents thrive in hypertufa. The container I'm most fond of in our garden, and the one most visitors seem to enjoy best too, is wide and shallow and contains a small piece of volcanic rock, several hen-and-chickens (*Echeveria elegans*), and an unidentified bronze-colored fleshy sedum that we bought off the plant rack outside the local hardware store.

Several years ago I started using hypertufa containers as planters for bonsai that were in the first stages of shaping and training. The containers are deeper, rougher and more unfinished than the elegant ceramic dishes usually used for displaying bonsai. But even if the hypertufa containers are untraditional, they somehow look appropriate. Perhaps it's because their texture brings to mind the rock and stone outcroppings found in mountain landscapes near the ancient trees that many bonsai are meant to evoke. At any rate, the fledgling bonsai are thriving in the hypertufa pots two years on, and the moss that bewhiskers the hypertufa surface has almost spread to cover the exposed tree roots.

Experiments with hypertufa

In addition to making planting containers, I've been experimenting with hypertufa stepping-stones. I use a strip of fiberglass 2 in. wide by 52 in. long to make a circular mold, much like a springform baking pan, then I set the mold on plastic-covered plywood and fill it at least 1½ in. deep with a fairly dry 1:1:1 mix, pressed down firmly. I drape plastic over the molded stepping-stone and leave it to harden for three or four weeks—if you want to, you can weatherize the top surface while the piece is still in the mold. At first I was curious about the strength of my stepping-stones, but set flush with the earth in my garden, they've held up fine for two years.

Although hypertufa usually is valued for its porosity, I've tried using it to make containers that hold water. In a spot that seemed just right for a tiny pond, I patted a 2-in.-thick layer of hypertufa against the walls and bottom of a hole dug 24 in. by 36 in. by 12 in. deep, then covered it with plastic and let it cure for several weeks. The results were mixed: The pond does look nice, as if a giant's hand had scooped out a hollow in some stone. But there was a seepage problem. I coated the inside of the pond with bentonite, a superfine clay that's supposed to be water-repellent. The pond no longer leaks, but the bentonite makes a sticky layer on the bottom of the pond, and it clouds the water a little.

I'm still puzzled about what factors determine whether a hypertufa container will hold water or not, but apparently the recipe and consistency of the mix make a difference. I used cement, sand and peat in a 1:1½:1½ ratio, mixed to cottage-cheese consistency, to make the pond. Since then I've made hypertufa birdbaths from a fairly dry 1:1:1 mix, which seems to work better. Finished birdbaths look pleasant when nestled under overhanging shrubs or at the base of a tree. I've also made water basins—relatively small containers, perhaps a foot square, with walls at least 3 in. thick and a rounded inner cavity. I sunk one basin about two-thirds deep into the ground in a narrow passageway filled with bamboo and ferns. The area now has the feeling of a small Japanese courtyard, complete with stone water basin. A pink camellia flowers nearby, and we float its blossoms in the basin every spring. □

Jan Kowalczewski Whitner designs gardens and garden ornaments in Seattle, Washington.

The Whitfords use Fibermesh reinforcement to strengthen the large rectangular and round hypertufa troughs in their Colorado rock garden. Here, a 15-year-old bristlecone pine shares a container with a white-flowering spotted saxifrage.

Tougher tufa
by Ernie and Jennifer Whitford

Our entire rock garden is planted in hypertufa troughs, both rectangular and round. To strengthen the troughs so that we can move them around the garden without breakage, and so that they'll withstand the repeated freeze/thaw cycles of a Colorado winter, we need to reinforce the hypertufa. We used to use chicken-wire reinforcement, but weren't satisfied with it for several reasons. Molding the hypertufa around the wire was an irritating and time-consuming process. The chicken wire didn't provide enough support to strengthen big troughs. Sometimes the hypertufa mix would chip or break off the corners or edges of a trough, revealing the chicken wire inside, and that didn't look good at all. Rock gardeners described these as the inevitable hazards of making hypertufa troughs, but we thought there had to be a better way.

It seemed that the best support for a hypertufa trough would be one that's part of the mixture itself. Then the support would be evenly distributed throughout the entire trough—as it is in carved stone. Our solution is a concrete reinforcing product called Fibermesh, sold by lumberyards and ready-mix concrete suppliers. (For the dealer nearest you, contact Fibermesh Company, 4019 Industry Dr., Chattanooga, TN 37416; 615-892-7243.) Fibermesh is easier to use than wire reinforcement, and makes troughs that are stronger and lighter in weight. In short, these troughs are perfect for our rock-gardening needs. Here's how we make them.

First we mix equal volumes of dry cement, perlite and sphagnum peat moss, adding 1 oz. of concrete dye per gallon of cement. (We're careful to wear dust masks and rubber gloves when handling cement.) We make large batches of this premix in a cement mixer and store it in 30-gal. trash cans, but you can mix smaller amounts by hand.

When we want to make a trough, we add Fibermesh to the premix at the rate of ⅛ oz. to ¼ oz. (about one big, fluffy handful) per gallon of dry mix. It takes roughly 3 gal. of mix to make a 15-in.-square trough. While mixing the Fibermesh with the other dry ingredients, we add just enough water to barely wet the mixture. It should end up about the consistency of cottage cheese.

We make the rectangular troughs in wooden molds that have wood putty inside the corners to make them round. For round containers, we make plastic molds by cutting the top 6 in. or so off 7-gal. and 10-gal. nursery cans. Our molds don't have bottoms, so we set them on a workbench covered with a sheet of plastic. We coat the inside of the molds with linseed oil before each use, to keep the hypertufa from sticking. Wearing rubber gloves, we pack the hypertufa tightly in place between the inner and outer molds of a trough. After the hypertufa has set for about ten minutes, we remove the inner mold and round the edges with a putty knife. Then we cover the trough with a sheet of plastic, and let it sit undisturbed for a full 48 hours.

Next we turn the mold over and slide out the trough. We use a screwdriver to carve finger-size drain holes in the bottom (and usually carve our initials or names there also). We brush the sides, top and corners of the trough with a wire brush, to bring out the texture of the hypertufa. Admittedly, at this stage, the trough looks like it's covered with cat hair. The Fibermesh sticks out on the sides, but we don't worry about that yet. For now, we move the trough to a safe place, picking it up by the bottom, not the sides, to avoid cracking it.

We cover the trough with plastic again and let it cure for a couple of weeks—the slower the cure, the stronger the trough. Meanwhile, we also want to leach out extra lime, so we use a hose to wash the trough from time to time. After the trough has cured for at least two weeks, we give it a final hosing, let it dry, and burn off the Fibermesh cat hair with a propane torch. We're careful to move the torch quickly, not holding it in one place for more than a second or two—the flame is so hot that any damp pockets left in the trough would explode, making small potholes. Once the Fibermesh has been melted off, the trough is ready to be planted and enjoyed for many years. □

Ernie and Jennifer Whitford garden in Colorado Springs, Colorado.

Building an Arbor
A simple design for an overhead trellis

by Barbara McEwan

Building an arbor is a rewarding project. With the barest minimum of carpentry skills, you can assemble an overhead support for climbing vines that will add beauty to your landscape and provide shelter from the summer sun. The design that my husband, John, and I came up with is very simple. You can easily use it as a starting point for an arbor that may better suit your own needs. The only constraint is that your arbor, like ours, be strong enough to bear the weight of the vines for years to come.

Some people build arbors for their decorative value, others build them for their shade. We constructed ours in self-defense. Our foes were deer, those lovely Bambis we all enjoy watching. But John and I wanted to see them somewhere other than in our little vineyard. Year after year the deer decimated the vines' new, spring growth, then returned to browse the shoots and leaves that the vines valiantly regrew. Because John was determined to have grapes, six years ago we finally decided to build an arbor.

An arbor can be covered with other types of vines, of course. You might consider such robust growers as Dutchman's-pipe (*Aristolochia durior*), silver lace vine (*Polygonum aubertii*), trumpet vine (*Campsis radicans*) or honeysuckle (*Lonicera*). Whatever you choose, take some time to learn about the vine's cultural requirements and growth habit in your particular climate. It would take several years for all but the most rampant vines to fully cover the arbor. You don't want to discover after all that time that the vine you chose is inappropriate for your arbor or for your site.

An arbor can serve as a landscape feature and as a refuge from the summer sun. The author and her husband built the arbor pictured above for these reasons, but also to lift their grapevines out of the reach of the hungry deer that often roam their property.

Siting and sizing the arbor

Although we built our arbor to put our grapevines out of reach of the deer, we also had to consider its role in the landscape. We have a number of ornamental and fruit trees grouped behind our house. The arbor, we believed, would fit into this grouping, yet its shape would set it apart from the surrounding trees, inviting a closer look. Big garden structures need settings to match. An arbor plopped down in the middle of a lawn or an open field would stick out like a sore thumb.

In siting the arbor, you should also avoid too much exposure to the wind. Vines in full leaf put any support under enormous strain. Gusty winds can be the straw that breaks the trellis's back. The site we chose for the arbor benefited from the sheltering positions of a nearby mountain, a forest and our orchard.

Because of the scale of our property, and because we wanted to grow plenty of grapes to eat, we chose to build a very large arbor, 8 ft. wide and 32 ft. long. In order to harvest fruit over the length of the grape-producing season, we decided to plant eight different cultivars. This in itself dictated a large structure because grapevines can be quite vigorous. Before deciding how many vines to plant, determine how much of the arbor one plant will cover.

Building the arbor

The basic design of our arbor is simple: four 10-ft.-long 4×4 posts sunk into the ground at the corners of an 8-ft. square are held in place at the top by 2×6s. Smaller-sized lumber, from 2×4s to 1×2s, adds structural strength and provides support for the climbing vines. (See the drawing on facing page.) To double, triple or quadruple the size of the arbor, put in two additional posts for each section and attach them to the first section with 2×6s. Our arbor is four sections long. Yours can be larger or smaller as your space allows.

To assure longevity, we used pressure-treated wood wherever possible. Because John was unable to find pressure-treated 1×3s and 1×2s, he coated these pieces with outdoor stain to help protect them from the elements.

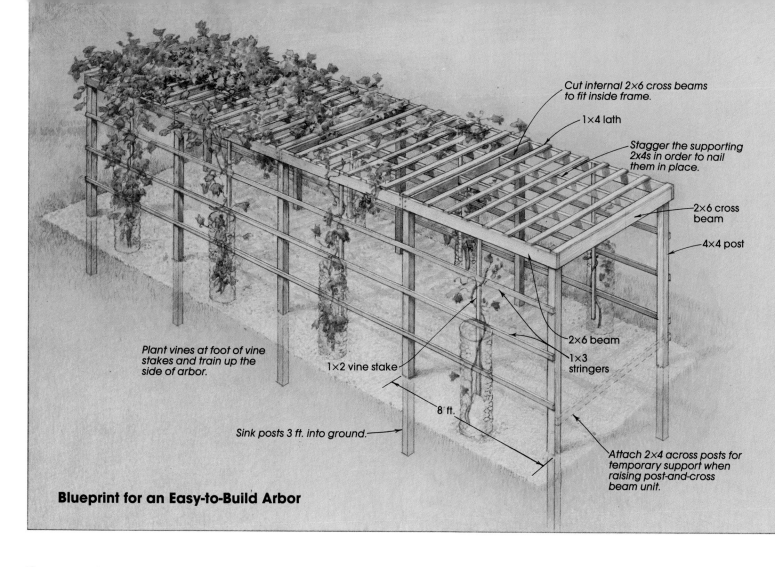

Cut internal 2×6 cross beams to fit inside frame.

1×4 lath

Stagger the supporting 2×4s in order to nail them in place.

2×6 cross beam

4×4 post

2×6 beam

1×3 stringers

Plant vines at foot of vine stakes and train up the side of arbor.

1×2 vine stake

8 ft.

Sink posts 3 ft. into ground.

Attach 2×4 across posts for temporary support when raising post-and-cross beam unit.

Blueprint for an Easy-to-Build Arbor

If you can locate treated 1×3s and 1×2s, by all means use them. (For more on the use of pressure-treated wood in the garden, see *FG #18, p. 68.*)

The first steps in the construction process are to stake out the location of the posts and dig the holes. For stability, we dug the holes 3 ft. deep, using a posthole digger (available from a local equipment rental company). Because we built the arbor on a slope, we had to cut the posts shorter on the uphill side so that the top of the arbor would be level and the posts could all be sunk 3 ft. into the ground.

We raised the posts two at a time. To do this, we laid them on the ground in line with the first set of holes. We attached a 2×6 cross beam to the top of the two posts with corrosion-resistant, zinc-coated, hex-headed screws turned by wrench into pre-drilled holes.

Next we nailed a 2×4 between the two posts about 4 ft. from the bottoms of the posts to provide temporary stability while raising the heavy unit. We lifted the posts, allowing them to slip into their holes. With a level, we shifted the posts until they were

vertical; then we backfilled the holes, packing the soil down tightly against the posts. (You can also fill the post-holes with concrete.) We then removed the temporary 2×4 brace.

We raised the next pair of posts as we had the first and attached the two pairs with a 2×6 beam and hex-headed screws. Before tightening the screws, we made sure the beams were level and the second set of posts was vertical. (It's easier to back out the screws and lift out the free posts to correct the depth or width of the holes than it is to lift out an entire section of the arbor.) We then backfilled the holes of the second pair of posts.

For additional support, we cut to fit two 2×4s and inserted them between the 2×6 beams, so that they ran parallel to the sides of the arbor. We nailed the 2×4s in place with 16d galvanized nails. Then we raised the posts for the next section, continuing as above until we had completed all four sections.

Once the basic frame of the arbor was finished, we laid 1×4 laths perpendicular to the 2×4s across the top. We fixed them in place with 10d

galvanized nails. We used six equally-spaced laths per 8 ft. section.

We wanted to give our arbor leafy sides, so we attached 1×3s horizontally to the 4×4 posts with 10d nails. These stringers provide support for the arms of the vines. We used two 1×3s on the uphill side and three on the downhill side. (Deer do nibble the side shoots, but the damage does not significantly affect the vines.)

To support the trunks of the young vines, we nailed a 1×2 vine stake to the stringers (using 6d galvanized nails) at each place where we planted a vine. These stakes run from the top of the arbor to within several inches of the ground, but they need not reach all the way to the ground. If the wood has not been pressure treated, such contact should definitely be avoided.

Our arbor stands today as solid as a boulder, and there's no reason why it should not stay that way for a long time. We're sure our vines appreciate it. Only the deer are losers. □

Barbara McEwan and her husband garden in Goode, Virginia.

Making an Artificial Bog Garden

Create a wet site for moisture-loving plants

by Walter Pickard

Several years ago I had a small formal pond installed in my backyard. Water lilies and fish thrived, but the pond lacked charm and character. I decided that it needed a bog—not a low, swampy place but a garden devoted to the interesting and attractive plants that thrive in constantly-wet soil. A bog, I believed, would soften the edges of the pond with lush foliage and make a good transition from the pond to the rest of the garden. But how could I hope to grow plants that love wet feet in our Virginia clay?

The solution came when my wife and I attended a garden symposium a few years later. One of the speakers talked about making an artificial bog garden by digging a hole, lining it with plastic and refilling it with soil rich in organic matter. She made it sound so easy that I immediately began planning a bog garden of my own.

Design

Choosing a site for a bog garden requires a little bit of thought. In general, bog plants perform best in a sunny or lightly-shaded spot. To give the garden a natural look, it's best to situate it in a low-lying area. You should also make certain that it's within reach of a hose. In my case, the pond site met all these requirements.

Let budget and site dictate the size of your bog. Some books recommend that a bog not be too wide because you could get a shoe full of mud while chasing a distant weed. In my experience, though, the dense growth of the bog plants shades out the worst weeds.

In designing your garden, think about the specific moisture needs of the plants you intend to grow. My aim

Lythrum 'Morden's Pink' brings height and radiant color to the bog garden in July and August. Although it does well in average garden soil, it thrives in a wet site.

was not to recreate a bog down to the last detail. I wanted, instead, to grow plants that love to have very wet feet side by side with more familiar perennials and annuals that like damp but not soggy soil. This allowed me a wider selection of plants and also helped to integrate the wet area into the overall scheme of our garden. In order to grow plants of varying moisture requirements, I made the bog deeper at one end. I planted the true bog plants in this area; plants that are merely moisture-loving went at the other end and along the edges.

Installation

Excavating the site for the bog and amending the soil was easy. I started by laying out a curved area around three sides of the pond, covering a total of about 150 sq. ft. To get natural-looking curves, I used a very high-tech design tool—the common garden hose. With a spade, I removed and discarded the grass. We are fortunate that the top 4 in. to 6 in. of soil in our garden is pretty rich. I removed this

good topsoil and put it aside on a sheet of plastic. Beneath the topsoil I found easy digging, mainly red, Virginia clay with few stones. I excavated 10 in. to 18 in. of this clay and discarded it, leaving a pit 14 in. to 24 in. deep.

To make the soil in the pit more water-retentive, I lined the pit with a double layer of heavy black plastic, readily available at hardware stores. (You can also use a pond liner; see Sources on p. 56.) I used up the better part of an 8-ft. × 50-ft. roll. I spread it across the bottom and up the sides of the pit, working it into the corners, pressing the wrinkles flat and cutting the edge to within an inch or two below ground level. With an ordinary four-tined garden fork, I then punched holes every 6 in. or so through the plastic in the bottom, so that the plastic would retain most of the water in the bog while allowing excess to drain into the underlying clay. This slow drainage would prevent the bog soil from getting too water-logged and rancid or sour.

Bog plants prefer a soil rich in humus. To increase the proportion of organic matter in my soil, I tossed all of the compost I had into the pit. Since this amounted to only an inch or two, I brought in about ten bales of peat moss to make up the difference. This plus the compost was enough for the approximately 150 sq. ft. of the bog. I mixed the peat moss with the reserved top soil, half and half, and filled the pit with this mix to within an inch or so below the original grade so that rain runoff would flow into the bog. I topped the soil off with hardwood mulch and filled it with water from the hose. With all that humus, the soil mix is springy and almost squishy under foot, just like a natural bog.

Planting

In planting the bog, I considered several things. First, as in the rest of the garden, I chose a selection of plants that

The author's bog garden surrounds his backyard pond on three sides, softening the hard edges of the pond and giving it a natural look. Although pond and bog make for a lovely combination here, you don't have to have a pond to justify a bog garden.

Organic mulch

50/50 mix of humus and top soil

Double layer of black plastic or pond liner

Pickard's bog garden extends lengthwise away from his den. To allow a view from the house of as many of the plants as possible, Pickard placed the tallest plants at the farthest end of the pond and smaller ones closer to his view. Pink lythrum and a yellow daylily add sparks of color to the lush foliage in the midsummer garden.

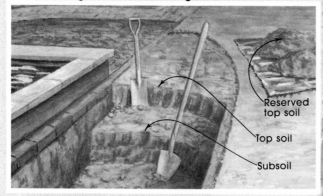

Reserved top soil

Top soil

Subsoil

Installing a bog garden

- **Remove turf** with a spade and discard.
- **Excavate top soil** (usually upper 4 in. to 6 in. of earth) and put to one side on a drop cloth or a tarp.
- **Excavate subsoil**, to an ultimate depth of 1 ft. to 2 ft., and discard.
- **Line pit** with a double layer of heavy, black plastic or a pond liner and punch holes for drainage.
- **Refill pit** with 50/50 mix of humus (compost and/or peat moss) and reserved top soil to within an inch or two of original soil level to encourage rainfall to drain into bog. (Pickard edged with bricks to help define the bog and to continue a motif used elsewhere on the property.)
- **Cover** bog area with organic mulch to reduce moisture loss and keep weeds down.

Illustration: Steve Buchanan

give us a steady succession of blooms and color throughout the seasons. I also considered the principal sight-lines by which the garden would be viewed. I planted taller, spikier plants farthest from view. The shorter plants, which I wanted to be more mounded and lacy for contrast, I put in the foreground. This may sound complicated and grandiose for an 11-ft. body of water, but it displays all the plants, and also keeps the pond partly hidden, inviting a closer look.

In the deepest and wettest portion of the bog, I planted the true bog plants: three pickerel rush (*Pontederia cordata*), one arrowhead (*Sagittaria latifolia*), three spike rush (*Eleocharis montevidensis*) and a lizard's-tail (*Saururus cernuus*). I ordered them from mail-order nurseries that specialize in aquatic and bog plants (see Sources below, right). I chose them for their lush foliage, to give the pond the jungly look that I wanted. Their flowers, for us, are a short-lived bonus. (For additional plants that like wet feet see facing page.)

The growth habits of these plants are interesting. As the ground warms up in April, the arrowhead and pickerel rush send up countless shoots that look a little like asparagus spears at first, but they rapidly form arrow-shaped or elongated heart-shaped leaves. These quickly fill the whole area with a solid mass of 2-ft.- to 3-ft.-tall foliage, followed by purple, upright flowers on the pickerel rush and white-petaled flowers on the arrowhead. Meanwhile, the lizard's-tail grows almost unnoticed among the other plants until suddenly, in midsummer, you see the long, furry, white flower that looks like a tail, though I'm not sure any real lizard has a tail this graceful. The spike rush has grass-like leaves which grow to about 18 in., and it produces an unobtrusive, brownish flower, like a small ball, in late summer. As the season advances, the spikes tend to fold in the middle and look bedraggled. I dislike the effect and have pulled out these plants.

To extend the blooming season, I put in widely-available perennials and annuals that either need damp soil or enjoy the extra moisture. For early color, I planted several Siberian iris (*Iris sibirica*) on the sides of the bog. I placed taller cultivars such as 'Cambridge' and 'White Swirl' to the rear, and shorter ones such as 'Pygmy Blue' and 'Snow Queen' in the foreground. Their different flowering times give us five to six weeks of bloom. Even after the blossoms have faded, usually by the end of June, the spiky foliage continues to be attractive.

For early summer bloom along the edge of the bog I tried a number of bellflowers (*Campanula*), including *C. rotundifolia* 'Olympica', *C. carpatica* 'Wedgwood Blue', and *C. glomerata* 'Joan Elliot'. Of these only the 'Joan Elliott' thrived, providing a welcome patch of dark blue, almost violet, color. Another perennial that grows well on the edge of the bog is the true geranium, or cranesbill. I've had good luck with *Geranium* 'Johnson's Blue' and

Lizard's-tail (*Saururus cernuus*) has bent spikes of white flowers in midsummer. The short-lived flowers are a bonus; Pickard chose the plant for the lush foliage that is characteristic of many bog plants. Lizard's-tail requires constantly-soggy conditions to thrive.

SOURCES

The following mail-order nurseries carry most of the bog plants described by authors Pickard and Gardner. All carry pond liners. The other perennials mentioned are available at garden centers and through a variety of mail-order nurseries.

Lilypons Water Gardens, P.O. Box 10, Buckeystown, MD 21717-0010, 301-874-5133. Catalog $5.

Maryland Aquatic Nurseries, 3427 N. Furnace Rd., Jarrettsville, MD 21084, 301-557-7615. Catalog $2.

McAllister Water Gardens, 7420 St. Helena Hwy., Yountville, CA 94599, 707-944-0921; 944-1850 FAX. Free catalog.

Paradise Water Gardens, 14 May St., Whitman, MA 02382, 617-447-4711. Catalog $3.

Perry's Water Gardens, 191 Leatherman Gap Rd., Franklin, NC 28734, 704-524-3264. Catalog $2.

Slocum Water Gardens, 1101 Cypress Gardens Blvd., Winter Haven, FL 33884-1932, 813-293-7151. Catalog $3.

The WaterWorks, 111 E. Fairmount St., Coopersburg, PA 18036, 215-282-4784. Catalog $2.

Wicklein's Water Gardens, 1820 Cromwell Bridge Rd., Baltimore, MD 21234, 301-823-1335. Catalog $4.

'Wargrave Pink'. They add nice color in June, with sporadic rebloom thereafter from the 'Wargrave Pink'.

For later color and more height, I planted *Lythrum* 'Morden's Pink' and 'Firecandle'. These flower through much of the summer and into the fall, and they provide additional height. A few clumps of *Liatris spicata* 'Kobold' have the same effect.

I have discovered that certain annuals tolerate wet feet. Vinca (*Catharanthus roseus*) and garden balsam (*Impatiens balsamina*) have performed well for us. The garden balsam will, incidentally, take over if not ruthlessly thinned in early spring, but its range of white, pink and almost-red blossoms is worth the trouble.

At the shallow end of the bog, in the shade of the magnolia, I planted astilbes. Their lacy leaves early in the season are followed by airy white, pink and red blossoms. The reddish-salmon *Astilbe × arendsii* 'Federsee', which flowers in July, and two cultivars of the pink, late-flowering *A. chinensis*, the low 'Pumila' and the taller 'Finale', have worked well in this location.

Together these plantings have softened and partially screened the pond's edges so that it looks almost as if it was created naturally. And that was the aim of the whole effort.

Maintenance

Maintenance of the bog is fairly painless. Depending on the amount of rain received, I might need to fill the bog with water once or twice a summer. I just let water from the hose run into the shallower end until it overflows at the lowest point. The flowering arrowhead and some of the other true bog plants tend to send out underground runners and can be invasive. But these sprouts are easily pinched off or dug out of the soft, damp soil with a trowel. I usually add compost and hardwood mulch in the late fall or early spring, and this, along with the shade cast by lush foliage, practically eliminates weeds in the area.

Our bog garden was inexpensive to make. I used approximately ten 4-cu.-ft. bales of peat moss, at a cost of about $60 when I undertook this project five years ago. The black plastic was $15. The plants cost about $225, and I probably spent 40 to 50 man-hours in the digging, hauling, mixing and planting, for a total investment of less than $300 and about a week's labor. Even if it cost half again as much to do the job today, I'd say that the results more than justify the effort. □

Retired Colonel Walter Pickard gardens in Alexandria, Virginia.

Some moisture-loving plants for the home garden

by Rob Gardner

Here is a short list of perennials suitable for bogs, streamsides and aquatic gardens in a home setting. I chose them for their foliage, flowers and dependability. Most of these plants are available at garden centers or through a variety of mail-order nurseries. You may need to order the irises and sweet flag from a bog plant specialist (see Sources at left). The USDA zone number indicates the approximate northern hardiness limit. All will fare well in most southern climates.

Irises (*Iris spp.*)

No bog or aquatic garden would be complete without at least one of the many beautiful and refined bog-loving irises. There are several species, hybrids or selections that should perform well in your area. As a rule, they grow and flower best in full sun and tend to bloom in late spring or early summer. Although happy in boggy, saturated soils, many of these irises will perform well in average garden conditions. Most do, however, require relatively high moisture levels during their blooming period. The following are three of my favorites:

Yellow flag iris (*Iris pseudacorus*)

Zone 5. This large European native has become naturalized in meadows, streambanks and marshlands in many parts of the eastern U.S. It has bright yellow flowers in early summer and grows 3 ft. to 4 ft tall. There are several nice selections including 'Alba' (whose flowers are, in fact, cream-yellow), double-flowered 'Flora Plena' and 'Variegata', which has yellow-striped leaves that mature to green.

Louisiana iris

Zone 4. This is a name given to a group of irises derived from several native species and their hybrids. Beautiful in both color and form, their flowers come in copper, yellow, crimson, royal purple and orange-red colors on stalks that reach 2 ft. to 3 ft. tall. There are many cultivars available.

Blue water iris (*Iris laevigata*)
Zone 4. A native of east Asia, this iris grows to 2½ ft. tall and bears beautiful, dark purple flowers in June or July. This species is especially well-suited to saturated soils.

Sneezeweed (*Helenium autumnale*)

Zone 3. Don't let the unfortunate name put you off. Long after most plants are past their prime in the bog garden, sneezeweed is just beginning to put on its show. Dozens of small, daisy-like flowers, usually yellow, mahogany, gold or a combination of these colors, open in August and September on upright 2-ft.- to 5-ft.-tall stems. Attractive selections and hybrids of *Helenium autumnale* include 'Butterpat', 'Crimson Beauty', 'Riverton Beauty', and 'Riverton Gem'.

Variegated sweet flag (*Acorus calamus* 'Variegatus')

Zone 4. Valued for its striking, sword-shaped foliage, which can grow 3 ft. to 5 ft. tall, variegated sweet flag makes a good screen or background for shorter plants. It forms an impressive clump of yellow-striped, vertical leaves. This foliage plant has inconspicuous flowers.

Cinnamon fern (*Osmunda cinnamomea*)

Zone 4. Many of the ferns belonging to the genus *Osmunda* thrive in soggy soil. The cinnamon fern is a vigorous, upright native that can attain a height of 3 ft. to 4 ft. If grown in constantly-wet soil, it will perform well even in full sun. (Native ferns are sometimes collected from the wild. Purchase only nursery-propagated plants.)

Japanese primrose (*Primula japonica*)
Zone 5. There are many primroses that thrive in moist soil. The flowers of this species open on candelabras that rise 1½ ft. to 2½ ft. above the basal rosette of paddle-shaped leaves. Flower colors vary from crimson to pink, purple and white, depending on the cultivar, but all appear in late spring. Japanese primrose is vigorous and easy to grow. It performs best in light shade.

Zebra grass (*Miscanthus sinensis* 'Zebrinus')

Zone 4. Many of the miscanthus grasses thrive in wet soil. This striking cultivar forms large clumps of arching, yellow-striped foliage that reaches 6 ft. in height. Zebra grass, along with the more upright *M. sinensis* 'Strictus', is unique because the variegated stripes run across the grass blade rather than parallel to the veins. Its conspicuous, feathery flowers develop in late summer. The persistent seed heads, along with the foliage, turn a tawny color after repeated frosts, adding interest to the winter landscape. (For more on the use of ornamental grasses in the landscape, see *FG#20*, p. 66.)

Rob Gardner is a curator of plant collections at the North Carolina Botanical Garden in Chapel Hill, North Carolina.

A Nature-Watcher's Window Box

Build a stage for hummingbirds and butterflies

Three tiers of containers and a trellis support nectar-producing plants that entice hummingbirds and butterflies to the author's windows.

by Harry Oakes

Outside my window, only a few feet away from where I stand, a hummingbird darts for nectar in a honeysuckle blossom; an elusive hairstreak butterfly settles on a strawflower. I can observe these beauties in such close proximity because I've created a window box stage for them. The box is a three-tiered frame that holds plastic tubs filled with nectar-producing flowers. I built the box to fit a particular window, but you can modify the design to suit your own needs.

What makes my window box unique are the plastic tubs I use as planters. They serve as units in a modular garden that I can change at will. If I want to experiment with different color combinations, I just rearrange the tubs. If a plant grows bigger than I planned, I can put a smaller plant in its place. Faded plants can be discarded and immediately replaced.

Designing the window box

To create your own bird and butterfly stage, first choose a large window, one that lets you enjoy the display. Butterflies hate wind and love sun. Most plants are sun lovers, too. So the best site for your window box is a sheltered, southern exposure. If you have a choice of sites, hang the box outside a window you pass by frequently so you'll have the best chance to see some action.

Three wood tiers form the main structure of the window box, which is strengthened with a surrounding trellis. The two upper tiers are actually frames that hold the individual planting tubs by their rims. The lowest tier has a plywood bottom, creating a trough for smaller containers. The window box is attached to the house, and wooden legs help carry the weight of the planted frame. You can build the structure from redwood, but I don't think that's necessary. I used number 2 grade white pine. (Because the legs sit on bricks, the wood doesn't come in contact with the ground.) The construction is simple—butt joints fastened with nails, glue and drywall screws turned into pre-drilled holes. Assemble the window box as a structural unit before attaching it to the house.

I attached the box to the wood-framed house with drywall screws. If you have a brick house, you'll need to use a masonry bit to drill holes for lead anchors or you'll need to attach wood strips to the side of the house with masonry nails.

I sized the top two tiers of the frame to hold 9x12x5-in. brown plastic tubs called Cambro Utility Boxes that I purchased from a local restaurant supplier. You can order these boxes by calling 800-833-3003 and asking for the supplier nearest you. The model is

Photo: Harry Oakes; illustration: Vince Babak

#912-CBP; the cost is about $5 each. Twelve of these small tubs are enough to fill the upper tiers, but I keep several more planted tubs on hand to replace plants that tire out. I fill the lowest tier with plants still in the market packs in which I bought them.

Drainage is important for plants in containers. So before you plant, use a ½-in. spade bit to drill three holes in the bottom of each tub and to drill a string of holes in the plywood bottom of the lowest tier. In the window box containers I use a soilless mix that is both fast draining and lightweight.

Choosing the plants

Choose plants that produce nectar abundantly. Hummingbirds and butterflies prefer different flowers. Hummingbirds favor the color red and use their long beaks to reach the nectar at the bottom of tube-shaped flowers. I've had good luck attracting hummingbirds with red salvia, bee balm and a hybrid honeysuckle called *Lonicera* x *brownii* 'Dropmore Scarlet', which I train up the trellis.

Unlike hummingbirds, butterflies like a place to perch while they feed. Flat, sky-facing flowers like daisies, strawflowers and asters suit them fine. While hummingbirds are here and gone in a flash, butterflies will stop to sunbathe if conditions are calm and warm. I encourage them to stay with a cake pan filled with fine aquarium gravel and water to the top of the gravel.

In my experience, nothing attracts butterflies like the butterfly bush *(Buddleia davidii)*. Planted in the ground below the window box, the butterfly bush feeds the butterflies while it screens the support legs of the frame. I've also had good luck growing dwarf buddleias right in the window box. The butterfly bush, which is hardy to USDA Zone 5, is widely available in a variety of cultivars, with colors ranging from white through pink to purple.

Maintenance

With the scale of the window box so small, maintenance is a small job, too. Watering is the only onerous task. Like most container-grown plants, those in the window box must be watered frequently—twice a day in hot weather. A regular sprinkling with a dilute solution of 20-20-20 fertilizer helps keep my plants looking their best. If a group of plants starts to flag, I just pop in a tub of reserves. At the end of the season, I dump tubs of annuals onto the compost heap. Perennials and woody plants, such as butterfly bush, can overwinter in their tubs, but I sink the tubs into the ground and cover them with mulch to avoid frost damage to the roots.

When the window garden comes alive, I find it a microcosm of the larger, natural world. Partly, it's a world I can control; partly it's a world I can only watch. But from this close viewpoint I see things I'd miss otherwise. □

Harry Oakes is an industrial designer. He gardens in southeastern Pennsylvania.

Building a nature-watcher's window box

The first step in constructing the window box is to size the structure to the window frame. Next, adjust the dimensions to accommodate the planter tubs. Assemble the three tiers of the window box, then attach the supporting legs and the trellis. Attach the completed unit to the window frame and the house as shown in the detail.

Attachment detail

Join window box trellis to house window frame or adapter strip of wood.

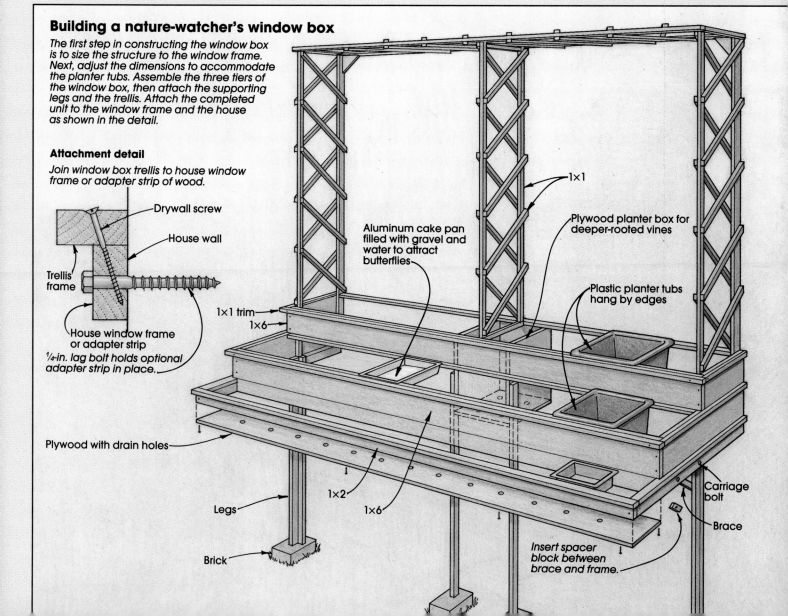

Drywall screw

House wall

Trellis frame

House window frame or adapter strip

¼-in. lag bolt holds optional adapter strip in place.

1×1 trim

1×6

Aluminum cake pan filled with gravel and water to attract butterflies

1×1

Plywood planter box for deeper-rooted vines

Plastic planter tubs hang by edges

Plywood with drain holes

Legs

1×2

1×6

Brick

Insert spacer block between brace and frame.

Carriage bolt

Brace

A Winter Shelter for Plants

An easy-to-build project that protects young and half-hardy plants from extreme cold

To shelter young and tender container plants, the author built a winter planthouse. Here, with 4x4 pressure-treated posts sunk to the frost line, he's backfilling the postholes with a soil/cement mix.

Sternberg drilled holes for carriage bolts to fasten tongue-and-groove pressure-treated 2x6s to the posts. In the background, the beam and the ledger fastened to the garage wall will support rafters.

by Guy Sternberg

very fall, I have container plants that are too small to go in the ground or too tender to overwinter outdoors in our Illinois climate. For years I sheltered them from the cold in a homemade plastic-covered wooden A-frame. This simple structure was inexpensive and adequate, but it was frustrating. It was too small—just 3 ft. tall, 4 ft. wide and 12 ft. long. I could barely crawl inside, let alone stand up, and I had to tilt tall plants on their sides, spilling potting mix and making it impossible to water them. Worst of all, once I had sealed the polyhut for the winter, I couldn't check the plants.

Last year, I finally bid farewell to the polyhut and built a solid winter planthouse that for a long time to come will take care of my ever-growing collection of seedling shrubs and trees, half-hardy herbs and perennials, figs, bonsai, potted bamboos, and nursery odds and ends purchased in containers at closeout sales (too late for fall planting). The design and construction of the planthouse are simple. Once you understand a few overwintering principles, you can readily make a version of your own to suit your site and plants. You may need a building permit, so check before you start planning.

Not a greenhouse

A winter planthouse is not a greenhouse. In a greenhouse, warm temperatures and sunlight keep plants growing through the winter. While a winter planthouse draws on ground heat and sunlight to stay warmer than the outside lows, even on frigid nights, it should still be cold—at or below freezing most of the winter. If the temperature is too warm, dormant plants may awaken prematurely, lose their hardiness, and suffer damage in a spring freeze.

Temperature aside, a winter planthouse protects overwintering plants in several ways. It blocks wind and sun. It holds humidity, which helps keep the soil in containers moist and prevents dehydration of evergreen foliage. And it keeps the plants safe from hungry rabbits and deer—a benefit as important as any other.

Designing a planthouse

You want a reasonably tight structure, to keep out winter drafts and to hold humidity. You want thermal mass inside to moderate the temperature. And you want a way to avoid overheating. The simplest approach is to keep the planthouse out of direct sun. As the drawing shows, my planthouse is a modified lean-to, a shape with headroom for me and my plants. The ends are sheathed with plywood, and the rest is covered with a sheet of white plastic, which screens some sunlight. The ground provides thermal mass and heat storage. A manual vent in one end controls overheating. I put glass panels in the end walls, and a large dial thermometer on a post inside. Without opening the access door, I can check the plants and the

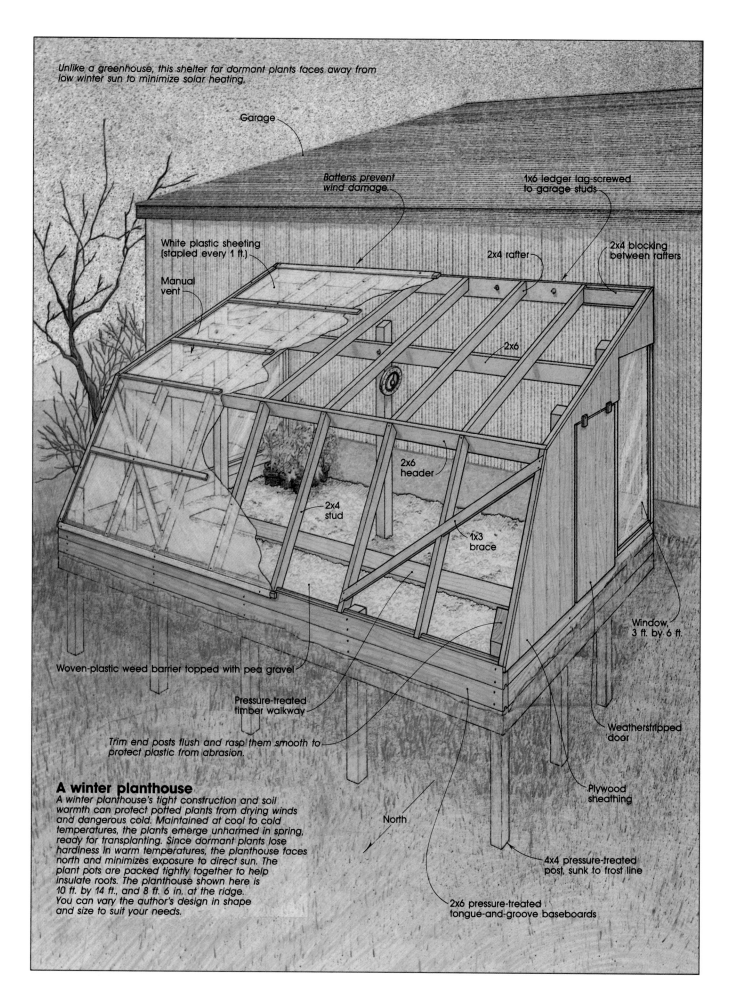

Unlike a greenhouse, this shelter for dormant plants faces away from low winter sun to minimize solar heating.

Garage

Battens prevent wind damage.

1x6 ledger lag-screwed to garage studs

White plastic sheeting (stapled every 1 ft.)

2x4 rafter

2x4 blocking between rafters

Manual vent

2x6

2x6 header

2x4 stud

1x3 brace

Window, 3 ft. by 6 ft.

Woven-plastic weed barrier topped with pea gravel

Pressure-treated timber walkway

Trim end posts flush and rasp them smooth to protect plastic from abrasion.

Weatherstripped door

Plywood sheathing

North

4x4 pressure-treated post, sunk to frost line

2x6 pressure-treated tongue-and-groove baseboards

A winter planthouse

A winter planthouse's tight construction and soil warmth can protect potted plants from drying winds and dangerous cold. Maintained at cool to cold temperatures, the plants emerge unharmed in spring, ready for transplanting. Since dormant plants lose hardiness in warm temperatures, the planthouse faces north and minimizes exposure to direct sun. The plant pots are packed tightly together to help insulate roots. The planthouse shown here is 10 ft. by 14 ft., and 8 ft. 6 in. at the ridge. You can vary the author's design in shape and size to suit your needs.

thermometer through the glass. When the temperature rises in late winter, I open the vent.

To minimize the risk of overheating, I built the planthouse against my garage, facing north. In winter, the structure receives very little direct sun. Building against the garage also allowed me to borrow thermal mass from the garage footing and a little insulation from the garage wall. The site slopes, so I dug a level floor for the planthouse. Cutting into the slope put some of the space below grade, insulated from wind and cold. To gain the same sort of insulation on a flat site, you could simply excavate the floor 6 in. or so and provide a drain.

I built the planthouse of CCA (chromated copper arsenate) pressure-treated lumber, since the constant humidity would cause decay in untreated lumber, except for redwood, cypress or cedar. The 4x4 posts that support the planthouse are sunk to the frost line (3 ft. here) and so have to resist rot and insects. All the lumber is treated to 0.40-lb. retention, the standard for wood in contact with the ground. The wood preservatives, salts of chromium, copper and arsenic, are tightly bound to the wood and cause no harm to nearby plants.

Construction

My aim was to finish construction in one weekend. The first day, I set the 4x4 posts. I laid out the 10-ft. by 14-ft. floor plan with stakes and string, and dug postholes. Then I mixed the excavation dirt 70:30 with portland cement, put the posts in the holes and backfilled with the soil/cement mix. As I worked, I repeatedly checked the posts with a tape measure and a level to make sure they were plumb and accurately located. With the postholes filled and tamped, I tied the posts together with a kneewall of 2x6s. I used what pole-barn builders call "center-match baseboards," which have a tongue milled on one edge and a groove on the other. I cut a trench in the slope for the first 2x6, leveled it, and spiked it temporarily to the posts with galvanized 10d

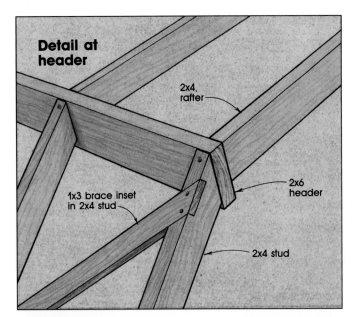

Detail at header

2x4, rafter

1x3 brace inset in 2x4 stud

2x6 header

2x4 stud

With rafters and studs in place, the author braces the planthouse against racking with let-in diagonal 1x3s. Here he's sawing notches in the studs so the 1x3 will lie flush with the edges of the studs and make a smooth surface for the plastic sheeting that's to come.

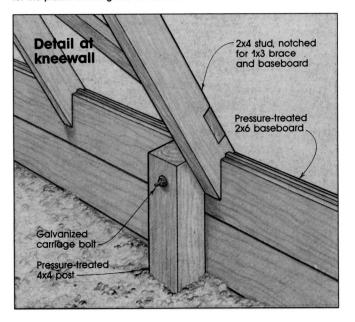

Detail at kneewall

2x4 stud, notched for 1x3 brace and baseboard

Pressure-treated 2x6 baseboard

Galvanized carriage bolt

Pressure-treated 4x4 post

nails. Then I nailed two more rows of 2x6s above the first row, and called it a day.

On Sunday, I started by installing beams. I leveled and nailed up the 2x6 beam that helps support the rafters, and nailed a 1x6 ledger to the garage for the ridge. To prevent drafts, I filled the grooves in the siding behind the ledger with silicone caulk. I ran lag screws 2 ft. on center through the ledger into the garage studs, and refastened the roof beam and the baseboards to the posts with carriage bolts. (All the nails and hardware for the project were galvanized.) I checked the measurements one last time, then retamped the backfill in the postholes and soaked it to set up the cement. (My soil was dry when I excavated. If yours is moist, the soil/cement mix will start to set immediately, so plumb the posts as soon as you backfill.)

With the posts and beams in place, I turned to the rafters and studs. I spaced the rafters 24 in. apart, measuring with care in case I decide one day to cover the planthouse with pre-cut acrylic glazing, or glass-paned units. I nailed a 2x6 header across the ends of the rafters to accept the studs, which slope and have angled ends. I fit each stud individually, notching the bottom end to rest on the baseboard and nailing the top to the header.

I finished the day with the last of the framing. To brace the structure, I ripped a 1x6 lengthwise into two pieces and nailed each piece at a diagonal in the corners. I notched the studs to let in the braces, so the plastic sheeting would lie flat against the framing. Then I trimmed the tops of the posts flush with the rafters and studs, and rasped the edges smooth to protect the plastic sheeting from abrasion. I framed in the ends of the planthouse with 2x4s and sided them with scrap plywood. Then I installed 3-ft. by 6-ft. glass panels salvaged from old patio doors. The glass is a convenience, not a necessity, but I like it. So much for day 2. Luckily, it was a holiday weekend—I still had Monday.

The next morning, I dug

out the floor, removing dirt until it was level. I covered the soil with a woven-plastic weed barrier, widely available at garden centers. The barrier allows water to drain but prevents weeds from growing. Then I laid a salvaged 3x12 timber down the middle of the floor for a walkway and spread 2 in. of pea gravel on both sides.

The finishing touches came next. I fashioned an access door from exterior-grade (CDX) plywood, with foam tape for weatherstripping. In the opposite end of the planthouse, I installed an adjustable vent. Then I checked the planthouse for cracks that might leak air, and filled them with silicone caulk. Supper was late that night, and I missed the Labor Day picnic, but I was done with carpentry. The plastic sheeting could wait.

I chose a dead-calm day in late October to install the sheeting. I used the cross-laminated white plastic that covers the planthouses of commercial nurseries. It's tough enough to take wind and snow loads for one or two seasons. You can buy the end of a roll from a local nursery, as I did, or order a full roll from A.M. Leonard, Inc., a general nursery supplier (P.O. Box 816, Piqua, OH 45356-0816; catalog free). I lugged my rolled-up piece up a ladder and let it unwind from the peak of the planthouse roof, stapling every foot or so into the rafters and then the studs. I worked alone, but I'd suggest using a helper to align and smooth the plastic, which, to prevent damage, should be as tight and wrinkle-free as a boot-camp bed. With the plastic stapled in place, I nailed 1x2s around the entire sheet, folded the plastic over them, stapled the fold to the 1x2s and trimmed the excess sheeting. Then I nailed 1x2s at intervals across the rafters and studs for extra insurance against flapping and tearing in winter gales. Some people staple a second sheet of heavy-gauge plastic or microfoam (bubbled-plastic insulation) on the inside of their planthouses. I don't need the protection, but in colder climates it's good insurance.

The planthouse is nearly complete. Plywood sheathes the ends. The author is test-fitting the weatherstripped access door, which remains closed most of the winter. The glass panel to the right of the door lets him check plants without opening the door. To control overheating, the planthouse was faced north and a hand-operated vent was installed in one end wall.

In the fall, the author covered the rafters and studs with double-reinforced white plastic sheeting and began to move plants inside. Lengthwise 1x2s across the rafters keep winter gales from tearing the plastic. Wrapping burlap around the tightly packed containers insulates plants on the perimeter.

The first winter

As winter neared, I brought in the plants. First, I sterilized the interior of the planthouse by spraying a 1:10 solution of bleach and water. I weeded the containers carefully, made sure each plant had a legible label, brought the pots into the planthouse, and jammed them together tightly to provide some cold protection for the roots, which are generally much less tolerant of extreme cold than the tops are. Then I drenched the pots with a mild fungicide and watered the pea gravel so it would keep the planthouse humid.

Before real winter, my wife, Edie, packed insulation around the last row of pots. (You can mound pea gravel against them instead—it's equally effective.) We soaked the pots again, closed the vent, and put up the thermometer so we would know when to start ventilating in late winter. Then we laid out some waterproof mouse bait (just in case the critters thought the shelter was meant for them) and closed the access door.

The planthouse performed as I hoped it would. With the outdoor temperature at -22°F, the planthouse thermometer read 5°F. I believe the temperature near the ground was probably close to freezing, fine for roots in containers. The coldest soil temperature I measured in the planthouse was 25°F.

If you need a winter home for marginally hardy or young plants, and have the most basic carpentry skills, as I do, you can build your version of my winter planthouse. My costs, helped by salvaged and leftover materials, were around $150. You might consider installing automated watering and venting. You might also consider getting a helper, even if you have a three-day weekend for construction. If you have a desk job (as I do) and are over 40 (as I am), take your time and avoid all those stiff joints and sore muscles. □

Guy Sternberg's home and private arboretum are near Petersburg, Illinois.

Kit Greenhouse Basics

Precut parts speed installation

Kit greenhouses like this one can be assembled speedily by a small crew. From foundation to glazing, this installation took two weeks.

by Jed Meuse

If you dream of having a greenhouse one day but are intimidated by cost or construction, my experience can help you. Like my father before me, I build greenhouses and solar rooms for a living. I'll take you step by step through the installation of a typical prefabricated kit greenhouse. A well-made kit is reasonably priced (about $50 per square foot, installed, excluding foundation) and can be put together by a handy person. Whether you assemble it yourself or hire a contractor like me, my experience will prepare you to recognize good practices. I have skipped some of the details of installation here, but kits come with manuals that even beginners can follow.

There are two basic greenhouse designs. One is a lean-to; it's higher on one side than the other and is installed as an addition to a house or other building. The other is an even-span—two lean-to's joined at the ridge—either free-standing or attached at one end to a house or other building.

Most homeowners build an attached greenhouse because the shared wall can save on construction materials, and since the shared wall is usually the north end of the greenhouse, it offers shelter from winter winds. An attached greenhouse also donates solar heat to the neighboring building. The kit I'll describe here is an attached even-span greenhouse.

The foundation

I lay out, account for and measure all parts in the kit before I start planning the foundation. Laying out a foundation usually takes adjustments to compensate for variations in the shared wall and the greenhouse components.

For stability, the foundation for a greenhouse must extend below the frost line (4 ft. deep here in New England). If the foundation settles or heaves during a freeze, the greenhouse frame will twist, causing the glass to shatter. Most patio slabs are poured to a 4 in. depth without footings and won't support a greenhouse.

There are several ways to construct a foundation. The most common method is to pour a concrete footing below the frost line and top it with a low wall of concrete, concrete block, brick or stone. For the job I'll describe, my client ordered a big greenhouse, 23 ft. 6 in. long and 15 ft. 9 in. wide (two Camellia 8, curved-eave models by Janco Greenhouses and Glass Structures that I attached at their ridges to form an even-span greenhouse). My client also wanted a 3-ft. high concrete wall faced with stone to match stone work on his home. The foundation would need to be 7 ft. tall (4 ft. below ground and 3 ft. above), so I hired a foundation contractor to form the walls. The manufacturer supplied a standard foundation drawing, which I altered to allow for the stone facing and for a heater, a cooler and vents. Some even-span greenhouses have a pole set on a footing to help support the ridge, but this kit had a glass partition under the ridge that formed a load-bearing wall and required a foundation. (The partition, which has a door, creates two rooms, one for cool-climate and the other for warm-climate plants.)

I'd hired an excavator to dig the foundation, but to my surprise, my client announced that he owned a backhoe and could do it himself. I laid out the foundation with stakes and string, and he dug a 4-ft. deep trench, making it 5 ft. wide so the contractor would have room to install the concrete forms. Next, the foundation contractor and his crew poured a footing 2 ft. wide and about a foot deep. Then they pushed 2-ft. lengths of ⅝-in. steel reinforcing rod halfway into the wet cement, along the center line of the footing. The rods lock the foundation walls to the footings. We let the footings cure, or air-dry, for a few days. Then the contractor poured the walls, and I inserted ½-in. x 8-in. anchor bolts (for the greenhouse sills) at 30-in. intervals. (See the drawing on p. 67.)

The foundation walls cured for a week, and then my client filled inside the foundation to within 8 in. of ground level with earth.

If you want a sink in the greenhouse, install a drain pipe and tie it into the main drainage system before you backfill. Compact the earth around

The author and a helper stand on scaffolding while they sandwich a structural I-beam between two half sections of the greenhouse. The greenhouse is also secured to a pressure-treated 2×6 sill plate and a 2×4 on the house wall.

the drain pipe to avoid damage and leaks from settling earth. Conduits for wiring should also be added at this time if you want the wiring to run under the floor. After filling with earth, I added 8 in. of ½-in. crushed stone inside to form a floor. The gravel provides drainage and easy access to water, heat and electrical lines.

I insulated the foundation by nailing serrated metal ties to the concrete and pushing 1-in. thick, rigid foam insulation onto the metal ties. Insulating the knee-wall with rigid foam keeps stone and cement, which are poor insulators, from conducting cold and dampness into the greenhouse. Enough of each tie remained exposed to anchor the stone facing to the concrete wall.

My helper, Bob Parker, and I prepared the top of the foundation by setting predrilled, pressure-treated 2×6s over the anchor bolts. Then I found the highest point of the wall with a transit, and shimmed the 2×6s to this level, with cedar shingles next to each bolt. I inserted the shingles, thin end first, from inside the wall, tipping the 2×6s slightly to shed rain and snow.

Once the foundation was ready, I prepared to assemble the greenhouse. I placed the aluminum sills on top of the pressure-treated 2×6s and took measurements. At both ends of the greenhouse, I checked the distance from side to side to make sure the sills were parallel. To check for squareness, I measured the distance between diagonal corners. I adjusted the sills until the measurements were the same, marked their position on the 2×6s and lifted them off. Then I caulked the inside and outside of the 2×6s where they met concrete, covered them, the insulation and the stone facing with aluminum flashing, and caulked where the flashing met the top row of sloped brick.

Assembly

The next step was preparing the wall of the house. Whether a greenhouse is framed with wood or with aluminum, it needs to be sealed where it meets the house. I attached pressure-treated 2×4s and flashing to the house to bridge uneven places in the wall and make room for the ridge vents to operate.

If a house is sided with clapboards or shingles, I remove a 4-in. wide strip, following the outline of the greenhouse gable. This exposes the house's sheathing, which provides a smooth face for the 2×4s. I slide the flashing under the siding and then nail 2×4s through

The author applies a strip of sticky glazing tape to the glazing bar (above). After peeling away the paper facing on the tape, he sets a pane of glass in place (below).

With the pane of glass in place and caulked, the author fastens a barcap over the caulking. The barcap secures the pane and keeps water, snow and sunlight off the caulking.

the sheathing into the house framing. (See the drawing on the facing page.) If your house, like my client's, is smooth brick, fasten the 2×4s to the brick with anchor bolts every 2 ft. Before you bolt the 2×4s in place, caulk their backs.

With the house prepared, I was ready to assemble the greenhouse frame. It's fastened together with bolts and screws, through predrilled holes. Following the manufacturer's directions, my helper and I easily fastened together each side in a day. We assembled the greenhouse in sections, on the ground—sill, vertical glazing bars (the parts that hold the glass) and ridge. Then my helper and I each lifted opposite sections and set them in place on the sill plate, ridges butted together. We sandwiched a structural I-beam between the ridges, bolted them all together and then anchored the aluminum sill through the flashing and into the 2×6s with stainless steel screws.

With the frame in place, we attached a horizontal brace, or purlin, across the midpoints of all glazing bars to provide additional support.

Glazing

My client's greenhouse now had a solid foundation and a sturdy frame, but it still needed glazing set into the walls and roof. Glazing can be plastic or glass. I prefer glass. Glass always looks great, while plastics eventually deteriorate. (For more information about glazing, see "Choosing a Home Greenhouse," *FG* #18, pp. 44-49.) Single sheets of glass work fine for unheated greenhouses or in warmer climates, but insulated glass is the sensible choice in a cold climate. Insulated glass consists of two panes with a space between them, sealed at the edges with caulking.

Installing glass is simple as long as the frame is square and level. A good kit comes with glazing tape, caulking and an aluminum barcap that creates a water-tight seal around each pane. Glazing tape is an adhesive putty, sticky on both sides. You unroll the tape and press it against the glazing bars. Then you position the glass carefully and press it against the tape. With the glass in place, you run butyl caulking along the edge of the glass and the glazing bar. Barcaps (see photo at left) hold the glass in place and protect the caulking.

I started glazing at the sill, completing one full horizontal row on each side of the greenhouse, then the next

Photos: Susan Kahn

row above, working my way up to the ridge. I alternated from side to side to keep the weight distributed evenly on the frame. The glass panes overlap like shingles, to shed water. The top row of glass on each side of the ridge forms vents. These vents have a separate frame that is hinged continuously at the ridge. Roof vents are needed in all greenhouses to vent hot, stale air.

Installing utilities

The greenhouse was now ready to have the utilities installed. For greenhouses, most codes require exterior-grade wiring connected to a ground-fault circuit breaker. A licensed electrician must do this installation.

An attached greenhouse can be heated by a home furnace. Consult a plumbing-heating contractor to determine if the furnace is large enough. If your furnace is inadequate, or if you're heating a free-standing greenhouse, install a forced-hot-air furnace or a boiler for hot water perimeter heat. I prefer hot water heat because it doesn't dry the air as forced-air heat can.

In summer, you must cool the greenhouse or circulate air. My client got an evaporative cooler, which has a fan that draws air through a constantly wet, porous mat. An evaporative cooler costs less to use than an air conditioner does and has the additional benefit of humidifying the air. However, it requires both electricity and a cold water supply. More economical alternatives include a gable exhaust fan controlled by a thermostat or an oscillating fan that runs constantly to move stagnant air.

Greenhouse benches are a matter of choice. My client built benches with tops of galvanized steel mesh framed with pressure-treated wood. They are easy to arrange and keep clean, and they also allow for air circulation. Factory-made benches are usually galvanized steel or aluminum.

The last things I installed were exterior roll-up shades to protect my client's plants from direct sunlight. Shades are easy to roll up or down, and can be made of shade fabric or more permanent, but more expensive, aluminum slats. Another option is shade fabric draped over the greenhouse roof, but it must be put on in the spring, and removed in the fall. □

Jed Meuse owns Meuse & Berglund, a greenhouse construction firm in Groveland, Massachusetts.

Illustration: Elizabeth Eaton

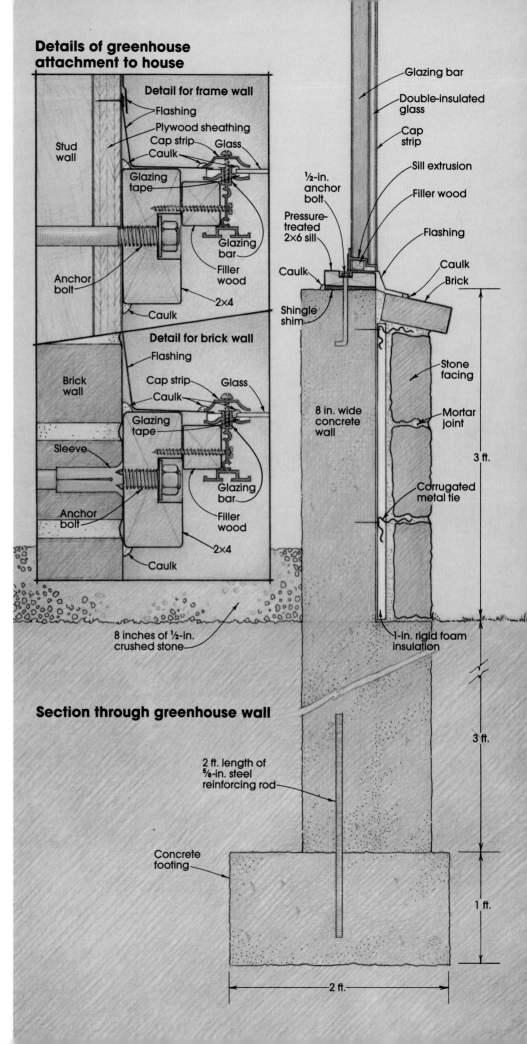

Screened by lattice and dappled with early shadows, a garden pond attracts a young admirer. A hidden outlet that channels overflow and a cleverly folded plastic liner keep the stone edges dry and firm.

Photos: Mark Kane

Garden Ponds that Work

New details control overflow and build reliable edges

by Earle Barnhart

eware of instructions for making garden ponds that extol the beauty of the water lilies but quickly pass over the details of construction. The flaws and shortcomings of typical construction soon lead to trouble. Since you have to invest time, effort and precious garden space to enjoy a pond, let me show you how to do it right the first time.

What's wrong with typical ponds?

Most of the instructions I've seen present pond construction in four simple steps. First, dig the pond, keeping the edge level. Then make a submerged shelf for water plants in containers. Next, line the excavation with plastic sheeting and fill it with water. Finally, cover the exposed sheeting around the pond with stones or soil.

I followed these instructions when I made my first pond. I dug the hole, put in the liner, and filled the pond with water. I placed flat stones to cover the edge of the liner in front and soil to cover it in back. Goldfish swam among the lilies, dragonflies sat on the irises, and ripples on the surface sparkled in the sun.

Over the next month or two, small, subtle things started to go wrong. First, it rained. The pond, already full, overflowed. In this case, an inch of rain sent 60 gallons of water over the lowest part of the edge, between two large stones. A few days later, an admiring visitor stepped close to the pond's edge to peer at a frog and drove those two stones into the soft, wet soil. More water drained through the new low point, exposing a few inches of liner around the pond. That's when I learned that a bare liner accumulates a persistent ring of dirt at the waterline. What's worse, the exposed liner is subject to deterioration—when direct sunlight hits the liner, it breaks down the plastic, which eventually will crack and leak.

My pond also had ecological shortcomings. I wanted a natural-looking edge with wetland plants on the banks and an abundance of aquatic life. Instead, I saw bare plastic, dry-land plants right to the water's edge, and a few plants in obvious, submerged pots. Even the portion of the edge covered with soil was a disappointment. The soil immediately became soupy mud that slid off the plastic and oozed into the pond. Worst of all, a visiting bird could find no shallow water to stand in for a drink or a bath.

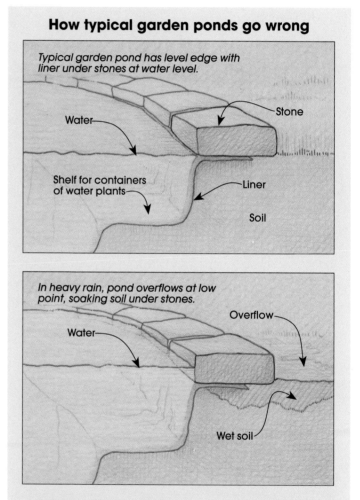

How typical garden ponds go wrong

Typical garden pond has level edge with liner under stones at water level.

Water

Stone

Shelf for containers of water plants

Liner

Soil

In heavy rain, pond overflows at low point, soaking soil under stones.

Water

Overflow

Wet soil

Someone steps on stones, or they settle on their own, and pond drains to new low point, exposing liner to degradation by sunlight.

Exposed liner

Water

Overflow

Wet soil

Illustrations: Elizabeth Eaton

Useful ideas from natural ponds

The flaws of my first garden pond prompted me to search for better construction methods. I read many books, observed public and private ponds, and collected every construction drawing and sketch I could find. But I've learned the most from looking closely at natural ponds.

Almost all natural ponds have banks that slope gradually into the water. The moist soil of the bank and the warm, shallow water at the edge encourage lots of life. Small fish hide among the plants in the shallows, insects tumble in and are eaten, a fallen log allows birds to reach the water safely or to rest in the sun. The many

Raising a capstone reveals the plastic liner, which runs under foundation stones, up behind them, and then folds back again.

A better stone edge for garden ponds

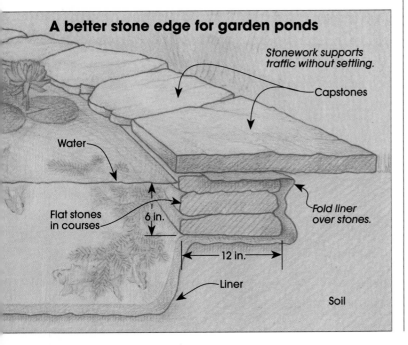

Stonework supports traffic without settling.

Capstones

Water

Flat stones in courses

6 in.

Fold liner over stones.

12 in.

Liner

Soil

species of plants, insects and animals in and around a natural pond interact ceaselessly, recycling wastes and keeping each other in check.

Finally, natural ponds have a store of nutrients and microorganisms in the mud on the bottom where wastes are recycled and nutrients are returned to the food chain. Many creatures winter safely in the mud on the bottom. I now avoid overcleaning garden ponds to protect this richness on the bottom.

In the past five years, with my partner, Hilde Maingay, I have built 20 ponds that draw inspiration from nature. The ponds have reliable edges and controlled overflow. They generally combine stone edges and sloping banks with outlets that channel overflow safely away from the edge. And they have a rich variety of life, in part because they offer many habitats, and in part because I bring in natural pond water and mud to get them started.

Better edges for garden ponds

I make two kinds of pond edges. Both offer many of the ecological virtues of natural ponds, and both keep direct sunlight from striking the pond liner. One is a stone-covered edge that supports people without settling while offering shelter to small fish, frogs and insects. The other, like a natural pond, offers a plant-covered bank and shallow water. (See drawings at left and on p. 71.)

For a stone-covered edge, dig a pond as usual, but make a shelf around the edge that is 6 in. lower than the final water level and about 12 in. wide. Then put in the pond liner, leaving a good 12 in. to spare all around the hole. Fill the pond just up to the shelf and then level the shelf exactly, using the water as a guide.

To finish the edge, lay several courses of flat stones on the shelf about 7 in. high and as wide as the shelf. Now, fold the liner onto the rock edge and backfill with soil behind the liner to firm it against the rocks. Finally, lay large, flat stones (capstones) on top to hold the liner and offer a place to stand. Trim any liner that shows.

My stone edge offers several advantages. For one, people can walk safely along the pond's edge, enjoying the sights, with their feet just a few inches above the water's surface. For another thing, no liner is visible or exposed to sunlight. Through the clear water at the edge of the pond, only stones are in view. What's more, the cracks and spaces between stones hide small fish, water striders, dragonfly larvae and other creatures that need a haven from predatory fish. The crevices also offer footholds for aquatic plants that need to be securely rooted, such as water celery (Oenanthe stolonifera) and parrot feather (Myriophyllum sp.).

For the other kind of pond edge—a plant-covered bank in shallow water—make the shelf 6 in. lower than the water level and 24 in. wide. Install the pond liner, fill the pond to within a few inches of ground level and then put a line of rocks or bricks around the inner edge of the shelf. Now pour rounded, ½-in. pea gravel on the shelf, sloping up from 2 in. deep at the inner edge to 8 in. to 10 in. deep at the outside edge of the shelf. Keep the pond liner upright as you add the gravel and backfill behind the liner with soil. When you finish, you should have a few inches of liner sticking up. Add enough water to put the gravel slope partly under water.

To finish the sloping bank, I spread an inch of soil on the gravel above the waterline and cover the exposed liner with humus (decomposed organic matter). The humus at the edge wicks water to plants higher up the bank. The last touch is a moss-covered log on the bank that slants into the pond, looking as if it fell ages ago.

A sloping bank supports a wide range of plants. In the shallow water, arrowheads and irises readily take root in the gravel. At the edge, water chestnuts and cattails thrive with some of their roots above water and some below. I set aquatic plants into the gravel either bare-rooted or with their roots in balls of soil. Many pond plants do fine in shallow soil and even pure gravel, getting most of their nutrients from the fertile organic sediment that continually settles to the bottom. The bank soon becomes a lush band of moisture-loving plants, spreading to locations most favorable to them. The gravel has one last advantage: when I move or divide plants, it's much easier to scoop up, wash and replace than the usual thick, sticky mud.

Overflow where you want it

No matter how you make the edge of a pond, you have to allow for overflow. I decide where to direct the overflow and then make the liner at that spot slightly lower than anywhere else. I recommend that you choose a point where the water will spill onto slightly lower ground or into a drainpipe leading to a lower area. There you can grow plants that tolerate occasional flooding.

Start work on the overflow once the pond is finished and filled. Raise the water level as high as the stone edge allows. Then form the overflow channel by lowering the liner about an inch below the water level for a width of about 6 in. In a gravel edge, carefully remove soil from under the liner to lower it, and remove some of the gravel on top to form a channel toward the low point. In a stone edge, remove a ledge stone to lower the liner and form a tunnel under the flat top stone and channel the water onto a lower level or into a drainpipe.

At the next rain, the pond will overflow into the channel and drain safely to lower ground. The edge of your pond will remain stable, and overflow will go where you want it.

New life for an old pond

If you already have a garden pond, there are steps you can take to improve its ecology and appearance. First, seed the pond with small samples of water and mud from natural ponds in your area. You'll introduce scores of new insects and microbes to enrich its ecology. Take the water from near the bank and take the mud from the bank and the bottom. I also try to collect small plants, complete with roots and mud, and transplant them into the pond. (Be sure you collect only those wild plants that are common and abundant.) As you introduce new species, create new habitats for them— slant a log into the water or set a pile of loose stones on a submerged ledge.

Finally, if you have the time and zeal, you can redo the edge of your existing pond and make an overflow. You'll have to drain the pond and redig the sides, but the reward is a more natural, more beautiful and more stable garden pond. □

Earle Barnhart designs and installs landscapes and ponds with his partner, Hilde Maingay, and gardens in Woods Hole, Massachusetts.

Gravel, water-loving plants and a half-submerged log make a natural bank for a garden pond, hiding the plastic liner. Here, birds drink and bathe.

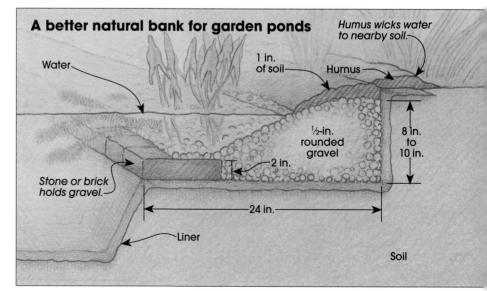

A better natural bank for garden ponds

Humus wicks water to nearby soil.

Water

1 in. of soil

Humus

½-in. rounded gravel

8 in. to 10 in.

2 in.

Stone or brick holds gravel.

24 in.

Liner

Soil

A cascade of small waterfalls and pools tumbles artfully over sandstone rocks and concrete, lending sound and motion to the author's hillside garden. The pink foxgloves at right tower over low rock garden plants.

Pool and Cascade
A beginner takes the plunge

by Des Kennedy

The sweet delights of running water in a garden have always attracted me. Whether minuscule or massive, a watercourse offers unique pleasures—the enchanting trickle of water over stone, the meditative calm of plants and sky glimpsed in a reflecting pool, the charm of songbirds splashing at water's edge.

Yet of all the garden projects I've longed to try, none seemed so intimidating as the watercourse that my companion, Sandy, and I eventually built with ease. We were daunted not by the scale of the cascade (a series of small waterfalls), nor by the amount of grunt labor involved, but by the challenge of capturing that elusive element, water, to make it give up its wild wanderings and behave according to human plans. And we were confused by conflicting information about design and construction from various "experts."

We learned in the making that a watercourse requires forethought in design and care in execution, but almost anyone can do it. Although our project might appear at first glance a tad grand for some backyard do-it-yourselfers, the spill of water and the pool are actually quite small. In any case, since the principles of making water features like these remain the same no matter what size project you're planning, you could easily adapt what we did to an even smaller scale.

Before you plan a water feature, do some research. We consulted books and magazine articles and encountered a bewildering diversity of opinion. Read whatever you can lay your hands on—but read each article as just one more opinion. Check your local

building codes. Finally, seek out the advice of people in your area who've had experience constructing a pool or cascade. Sandy's father had constructed a lovely miniature cascade a few years back. He provided helpful hints as well as an example to follow and thereby prove myself a fellow worthy of his daughter.

Choosing a site

There are several things to consider before you site a water feature. Try to keep it near the house so you can enjoy the sight and sound of water at all hours. There you'll have ready access to electricity for the pump and to water for filling the pool. If you plan to grow aquatic plants, which require full sun for blooming, avoid heavily shaded sites. Steer clear of overhanging deciduous trees—cleaning their fallen leaves out of the water every autumn is a nuisance.

For us, siting was a simple matter since we had a small hillside—about 8 ft. in vertical drop—close to the house. We decided to develop a rock garden on the hillside and have a small cascade thread its way through the rocks, with short waterfalls spilling into small pools and finally into a larger pool at the bottom.

If you're not blessed with a hillside but still want a cascade, you can create an artificial grade. Even a small spill can be very effective, and you can create it with no wasted effort by mounding up the earth excavated from the pool. For a larger hill, start with rock or rubble and cover it with earth.

Design inspired by nature

Nature is a marvelous instructress. A few hours spent contemplating the spill of water along a brook near our home revealed the secrets of how water cascades over stone, hollows out small pools, undercuts banks and glistens over gravel. Soothed by the

beauty of water and excited by its possibilities, we decided to have our cascade meander and trickle down the hill rather than drop dramatically and noisily, and to make it look as if it had occurred naturally, rather than by human contrivance.

It's important that the scale of the cascade—the volume of water and the size of the pools along it—is appropriate for the size of the hill, the rocks you use and nearby plantings. A tiny trickle can disappear among huge boulders, large shrubs and trees. Similarly, an aggressive torrent will overwhelm alpines or other miniature plantings. I don't believe there's a rule of thumb for figuring proper scale—you must rely on intuition, common sense and the lessons of nature. Because our cascade runs through a rock garden planted with small plants, we opted for a low-volume water flow.

Scale also affects cost. A cascade like ours needs a pump to lift water from the bottom to the top of the watercourse. The higher the lift and the more water running in a cascade, the larger and more expensive the pump.

Apart from the question of apt proportion, there are some other considerations. Several small waterfalls of different heights create an interesting diversity in the "soundscape," more than one or two loud splashers would. Above all, if young children frequent the area, you should fence it off or keep a close eye on them.

We made the bottom pool about 6 ft. in diameter—just large enough for water gardening if we decide to take it up. If you plan to include fish or aquatic plants in your pool, make it 18 in. to 24 in. deep. Deeper pools can be designed with edge shelves or islands about 18 in. below water level on which tubs of water lilies can be placed. Most aquatic plants prefer relatively calm, warm water. You can't expect them to thrive in a pool that

This view from the top of the cascade shows a spillway and several small pools lined with plastic and newspaper. The author is pouring sandstone-colored concrete on the plastic of the lowest small pool.

for the water; on others I had to undercut the lip of the overhang to prevent the water from running back along its underside.

I lined the pools and the spillways between them with three layers of material—first newspaper, then heavy plastic and finally a topping of concrete 2 in. thick. The newspaper protects the plastic from punctures, and the plastic prevents leaks. I extended the plastic several inches onto the overhanging rock at each waterfall and applied a sealer to the set concrete. With more bucketsful of water, I tested the splash of each waterfall to ensure that the receiving pool was wide enough.

I outlined the shape of the bottom pool with a piece of thick rope and set to digging. Unfortunately, in my zeal to have the pool appear natural, I included so many squiggles and wiggles that the excavation looked more like a piece of a jig-saw puzzle than anything from nature. A few more hours of work produced a gently curved hole about 2 ft. deep in the center with gradually sloping sides.

A pool that holds water

Despite the false start, digging the hole was a simple matter compared with the agony of trying to decide how to waterproof the pool. The fundamental choices are concrete, prefabricated fiberglass, and plastic sheeting (also called pool liner). Concrete pools require considerable skill and labor, and if improperly constructed, especially in a climate where the ground freezes, are prone to cracking. Fiberglass shells are durable and idiot-proof, but they're also rather pricey and look unavoidably artificial. (Prefabricated fiberglass cascade pieces are also available, with the same pluses and minuses.) Plastic sheeting is relatively inexpensive and easy to install, impervious to freezing and not glaringly artificial-looking. But pool liners are also easy to puncture and have a limited life-span—between ten and 40 years, depending upon their thickness.

I chose a pool liner. A simple formula determines the required length and width of the liner. Add twice the depth plus twice the edge detail (a minimum 6 in. overlap at pool edge) to the length and to the width of the excavation. At 10 ft. sq., my 20 mil PVC pond liner cost just under $85 (in U.S. dollars). Some pond supply companies will make up a liner to your specifications. It's more expensive, but it fits more snugly.

is frothing from a torrent. To accommodate both a cascade and aquatic plants, you'll need separate pools or a single pool large enough to absorb a cascade at one end while remaining calm at the other.

Waterfalls where you want them

We began construction by moving earth around the hillside to about the contours we wanted. Next I buried a section of 1½-in. diameter black polyethylene water pipe, running it from the location of the bottom pool to the top of the hill. Through it, I would insert—and remove for repairs, if nec-

essary—a ½-in. diameter polyethylene pipe to carry water from the bottom pool to the top pool.

I started building the cascade from the bottom and steepest part of the hill, making three small waterfalls and pools almost directly above one another. Higher up, the grade lessened, and I included a short, 4-in. deep spillway between each waterfall and pool.

I constructed each waterfall with a flat, overhanging rock and then poured a bucketful of water along the watercourse to see how it would spill from the overhang. With certain stubborn rocks I had to hand-chisel a pathway

Before laying the liner, we precisely leveled the pool edges to prevent creating an unsightly patch of exposed pool liner on the high side. We also removed sharp stones from the excavation and lined it with a 1-in. thickness of newspaper to protect the liner against puncturing. (A thick layer of sand works, too.) Then we unfolded the liner in the pool, allowing it to relax into the contours. After anchoring the perimeter of the liner with heavy rocks, we filled the pool with water to compress the liner into all the corners of the excavation, gently spreading and smoothing out bulges in the liner by hand. I trimmed the corners and stored the excess for possible future patches. Then I laid large sandstone slabs around the pool perimeter so they covered the liner edge, using rocks that could overhang the edge without tumbling in.

Selecting a pump

Choosing the right pump for our cascade was easy. Pump dealers or water garden suppliers carry an assortment of small, submersible pumps specially designed for water gardens. They're rated by gallons-per-minute and vertical lifts. To figure the flow I needed, I put a garden hose at the top of our cascade and played with different volumes of water until I found a pleasing rate. Then I stuck the hose into a five gallon bucket, timed how long it took to fill the bucket and divided the time by five to get the gallons-per-minute.

I tucked our pump beneath an overhanging rock on a raised shelf of soil that I made when I was excavating. (The pump works best if it's not at the pool bottom, where debris collects.) Also, the pump is easily accessible for repairs and removal.

Mixing electricity and water can be a high-risk business, and you should take particular care to follow the safety guidelines that come with your pump. A pool is no place for some haywire extension-cord arrangement. We hired an electrician to run a power line through a protective piece of underground pipe from the house electrical panel to a poolside receptacle for which I fashioned a small, concrete, waterproof housing. We protected the line with a ground-fault interrupter (GFI), which automatically cuts off electricity when there's a voltage leak. You can buy a GFI (which is required by the U.S. National Electric Code) from your local electrical-supplies dealer.

The author checks a groove that he just chiseled in the rock to the left of his hand. The sharp lip of the rock sends water falling cleanly onto the spillway just below.

After what seemed like months of planning, heaving around rocks and earth, hard decision-making and experimentation, the day at last dawned when our cascade and pool were completed. We plugged in the pump. We waited, trembling with anticipation, and yes, there it came: a tentative trickle, then stronger, growing to a boisterous splashing and gurgling, a playful, exuberant, lovely little cascade, tinkling and whispering through the garden. What fun! We pictured ourselves reclining lazily by poolside during the dog days of summer, soothed, refreshed and rewarded by the sweet, cool splash of water. □

Des Kennedy gardens on Denman Island, British Columbia, Canada. He is the author of Living Things We Love to Hate *(1992, Whitecap Books, Vancouver, BC, Canada).*

Seen up close, small waterfalls seem to spring from the rocks. A green-and-white hosta in the foreground provides a bright focal point amid the many shades of green and the small flowers of the rock garden.

Building a Lily Pond
Shovels, friends and a patch of PVC create a backyard oasis

by Ed Nichols

The ancient, multi-trunked fig tree behind our house was becoming an eyesore, a profusion of dead stumps and undesirable volunteers. Removing it was a painless decision, but we were uncertain about a replacement. My wife, Mindy, and I wanted something that would require minimal maintenance and preserve the view from our kitchen, previously blocked by the fig. We also wanted to try something different. After considering various options, we agreed on a lily pond.

We wanted to build the pond ourselves, but knew very little about how to construct or maintain one. A pond, being permanent, would be very unforgiving of our mistakes, so we consulted Felder Rushing, our extension horticulturist, and Allen Burrows, a landscape contractor who had recently installed a large lily pond. They assured us that the project was feasible: With their help, we could design, hand-dig and install a small pond, 8 ft. by 15 ft., over a series of weekends without draining our energy or our bank account. Here's the story of what we did and what we learned.

The first, and most important, consideration in pond building is keeping the water in the pond. Before the advent of fiberglass and PVC liners, small ponds were most often made of reinforced concrete. Concrete permits flexible design, but is expensive and difficult for a novice to work with. In addition, our highly expansive yazoo-clay subsoil swells and shrinks considerably with groundwater changes, so concrete would have required extensive reinforcement to keep it from cracking and leaking. Premolded fiberglass shells are much easier to install than con-

There are faster ways to excavate a small pond, but shovels are doubtless the cheapest. Ed Nichols and a few friends dug his in a day (above). The three levels were designed to accommodate different aquatic plants.

crete, but cost about five times as much as a PVC liner and restrict the choice of shapes. Thus, we rejected the other alternatives and elected to use a PVC liner.

A PVC liner is a sheet of durable plastic about as thick as a truck-tire inner tube. It's easy to install (dig a hole and drape the liner in it), and it's impervious to roots and unappetizing to burrowing critters. If inadvertently sliced or punctured, it can be patched much like a bicycle tire. Its main natural enemy is ultraviolet light, which degrades the plastic. But, protected somewhat by the water, a PVC liner should last at least ten years. PVC ponds can be made any shape, and for a moderate price. Our off-the-shelf, 13-ft. by 20-ft. liner cost about $200; custom-cut sizes are more expensive.

Our design was straightforward: a pleasing, curved outline, and three levels to accommodate the aquatic plants we wanted, which needed to be planted at specific depths to mimic their natural habitats. Water lilies would grow in the deepest water and bog plants (equisetum, iris, pickerel rush) on the ledge. The intermediate level gave us an option for future plantings. And, of course, we intended to stock the pond with some colorful fish.

The right combination of aquatic plants (with or without fish) can keep pond water algae-free and clear. We added a small electric pump to circulate the water gently for the fish, and to allow us to drain the pond periodically for cleaning. A drainage system channels overflow rainwater through piping into the adjacent yard. We decided on simple landscape devices to tie the pond into the surrounding yard. The pond is edged with flagstone, which extends into a patio sitting area on one side; a small landscaping berm borders the other side, hiding the drain tiles and breaking the flat expanse of our yard.

To prepare the site, Felder and I removed the half-dozen or so fig trunks, severing the lateral roots with an ax, then pulling out the trunks with my tractor and a chain. We hadn't drafted precise plans on paper, so we simply outlined the pond on the ground with a garden hose to get just what we wanted. Then our six-person pond crew began the excavation, first digging to 8 in., the depth of the ledge. This was relatively easy because it was early spring and our soil was still moist. (If in your area the ground is dry, soak it until you can dig readily, but not so much that soil sticks to the shovel.) Next, gauging the width of the ledge by eye, we dug the shallow and deep ends, 16 in. and 24 in., respectively. On our flat site, we wanted the water and the ground to be on about the same level, so we leveled the banks, checking them with a 4-ft. spirit level at-

tached to a longer, straight board. We also leveled the ledge so that we could put the bog plants at a uniform depth.

For drainage, we used clay drain tiles, 7 ft. long and 4 in. in diameter, left over from an earlier building project. PVC pipe would also work. The diameter isn't critical; it will only need to handle rain runoff. We placed the tiles as shown in the drawing on p. 79, taking advantage of the natural slope away from the pond, and leaving room for a drainstone and sloped concrete pad, which direct water into the tiles. Then we banked up soil from the excavation—primarily topsoil mixed with some subsoil—on top of the tiles and on two sides of the pond to form the landscaping berm. The soil was moist enough to stay in place; dry soil might need to be watered as it's piled up to settle it. Cottonseed hulls used as mulch after planting did a fairly good job of preventing soil from washing off the berm.

To prevent any sharp objects from puncturing the liner from underneath, we removed all protruding rocks and sticks from the excavation. Then to cushion the liner, we spread a ½-in. layer of clean builders' sand on each level, covered that with several sheets of newspaper, and laid down a layer of old sheets and bedspreads. This may have been overkill, but we haven't had any punctures yet.

Next we spread the liner, a 32-mil (0.032-in.) black PVC pond liner ordered from Lilypons Water Gardens (see Sources, p. 80). A 20-mil liner would also have worked, but since the cost was about the same, I bought the thicker, stronger one. (Thin plastic can crack in colder climates, so be sure to use plastic 16 mil or thicker.) I had calculated the liner size from our rough plans, long before we dug the pond. To figure its length, I added the pond's longest dimension to twice the maximum depth, and allowed an extra 2 ft. to provide a 1-ft. flap of plastic to tuck under the flagstone edging. By a similar calculation I determined the width. Because our pond would vary in shape and depth, I had guessed that we could get away with an off-the-shelf liner slightly smaller than the theoretical dimensions. At the moment of truth, we were all relieved to see that the liner fit.

Anchoring the overhanging flaps with bricks, we began the slow process of filling the pond with water from a hose. As the pond filled, we gently pulled on the liner to work it into the contours of the excavation. When doing this, we smoothed out the plastic as best as we could. A few wrinkles are inevitable, but don't really matter—water pressure will snug up the liner nicely against the pond walls. The water was also our best indicator of how level the ledge was—where necessary, we reached under the liner to shore up the ledge by adding or scooping out a little

To protect the liner from punctures, Nichols first spread ½ in. of sand on the pond floor, then layered on newspaper and bedspreads.

As the pond was filled with water, the liner conformed to the contours. Nichols and helpers shifted soil beneath the liner to level the ledge.

Allen Burrows set the flagstone perimeter in mortar. The liner is held in place under the flags.

soil. Finally, we trimmed the PVC in places where it overlapped more than 1 ft., leaving enough to be held firmly under the flagstones. We saved the extra PVC in case future repairs are needed. By the end of the first day, the pond was filled to the top with water, the liner fit well and all was ready for laying the flagstone.

We chose Tennessee flagstone for its availability and low cost—the ton of 1-in.- to 1½-in.-thick stones we bought came to $175. Allen recommended laying the stones in a bed of mortar, 2 in. to 3 in. thick. Although we could have laid the flags without mortar on a sand or soil base, a mortar bed keeps them level and inhibits weed growth. We didn't reinforce

In the finished pond, bricks serve as plant platforms. The drain tiles visible at upper right channel overflow rainwater. The pond is shown being refilled after its first spring cleaning.

adjacent flags. We followed behind Allen, removing ⅛ in. to ¼ in. of mortar from the top of the joints, outlining each stone. Then we smoothed the joints with a pointing trowel and sponged off the surface of the stones. In the mortar under one of the stones, we laid a 1½-in.-dia. conduit for the pump cord. Later we set the posts for the sheltered sitting area and laid the stone for the patio.

We installed the pump before planting the pond. Our plants and fish would do fine without a pump, but since fish prefer moving water, we bought a small pump—the ⅟₁₆₀-hp "Little Giant" from Lilypons. It pumps only 100 gal. of the 1300 gal. in the pond every hour, but works fine for creating water movement. For large fish, you might want to oxygenate the water; if so, you'll need to lift the water into the air through a waterfall or fountain and will probably need a pump with a larger capacity. Although we rely on a plant, anacharis, to filter the water, pump-powered filters can also remove suspended particles. For this purpose, the pump should have the capacity to recirculate 50% of the volume of pond water every hour. Water lilies like still water, so we located the pump at the shallow end, and we elevated it on a flagstone to minimize clogging from debris that accumulates on the pond bottom. We run the pump constantly for the fish, and the water movement helps prevent possible freeze-over in the winter.

Pumps for use in water are sealed and grounded, and contain a circuit breaker that automatically cuts off electricity if current exceeds the capacity of the wiring. Occasionally, damage to the cord or pump may result in low-voltage power leaks that don't activate the circuit breaker, so as added insurance we wired the pump to a ground-fault circuit interrupter, which cuts off power when there's a low-voltage leak.

Once the pump was in place, we attached a ½-in. hose to it, removed the dirty water from the pond and cleaned the liner. Then we refilled the pond with fresh well water. Chlorinated water can harm plants and fish, so if your supply contains this element, let the pond water sit for 24 hours before planting or stocking to allow the chlorine to evaporate.

A pond should be able to support as many plants as can fit in it, but we used only a few, as we wanted to see our fish and avoid an overcrowded effect. When selecting plants, remember that bog plants grow upright, occupying space roughly the size of their container. Water lilies spread from 1 sq. ft. to 12 sq. ft. or more, depending on the variety. Friends donated many of our bog plants: umbrella palm (*Cyperus alternifolius*), dwarf cattail (*Typha minima*), and several types

the mortar with wire, and we haven't had a crack in two seasons. But in colder climates, frost heaving might be a bigger problem and necessitate bed reinforcement. Allen's mortar recipe consisted of two bags plus three extra shovel scoops of Sakrete masonry cement, four shovelfuls of sand, and one-half shovelful of portland cement. We added water until the mixture was stiff enough to stay in a mound; no standing water was present, but the mix wasn't crumbly. Mortar for 100 sq. ft. of flagstones required 15 bags of Sakrete cement and three bags of portland cement. We mixed the batches in a 3-ft. by 6-ft. mortar box, a real help if you're mixing a lot.

It was easiest to lay the stones on the perimeter while standing in the pool, so we bailed out about 6 in. of water to prevent sloshing. Then we scraped away grass from the soil and added or removed soil under the overlapping liner to level the perimeter. We set the drainstone first, mortaring a flagstone in at the water level, one stone's thickness lower than the other flags. Next we poured the sloped concrete pad between the drainstone and the drain tiles. With this done, Allen moved around the perimeter, selecting and setting the odd-shaped stones in mortar directly on the overlapping PVC and surrounding soil.

The stones overhang the pond's edge by approximately 2 in. to hide and protect the PVC. Mortar in the joints bonded

Photos: above, Ed Nichols; facing page, Tom Roster; drawing: Elizabeth Eaton

Nichols' completed lily pond affords a cool, serene spot in the yard. Water lilies and bog plants provide a long season of bloom.

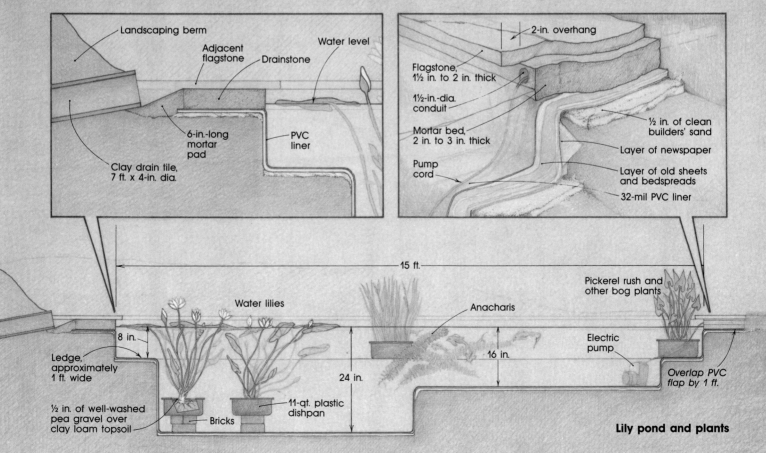

Landscaping berm

Adjacent flagstone

Drainstone

Water level

6-in.-long mortar pad

PVC liner

Clay drain tile, 7 ft. x 4-in. dia.

2-in. overhang

Flagstone, 1½ in. to 2 in. thick

1½-in.-dia. conduit

Mortar bed, 2 in. to 3 in. thick

Pump cord

½ in. of clean builders' sand

Layer of newspaper

Layer of old sheets and bedspreads

32-mil PVC liner

15 ft.

Water lilies

Anacharis

Pickerel rush and other bog plants

8 in.

16 in.

Electric pump

Ledge, approximately 1 ft. wide

24 in.

Overlap PVC flap by 1 ft.

½ in. of well-washed pea gravel over clay loam topsoil

Bricks

11-qt. plastic dishpan

Lily pond and plants

Cold-weather ponds

In colder climates where pond water freezes, water lilies, bog plants and fish need special care. According to Charles Thomas and Anita Nelson of Lilypons, even if you have chosen the hardiest plants for your conditions, their roots need to be protected from freezing and to be kept moist. If your pond doesn't freeze all the way to the bottom, it's best to overwinter the plants in the pond, insulated by the ice layer. After a killing frost, cut back the foliage and place the plants on the pond bottom.

Fish can adapt to living in an ice-covered pond by slowing down their metabolism, but they still require oxygen. If ice covers the pond surface for more than one week at a time, the buildup of gases from respiration and decomposing organic matter can be toxic to the fish. Since the fish will undergo stress if moved inside to an aquarium, it's better to leave them in the pond and let gases escape through a hole melted in the ice with a pond deicer, a thermostatically controlled heating element on a flotation device, available from pond suppliers.

If deep ice endangers the plants or the fish, they should be taken out of the pond. Remove old lily pads and above-ground growth of bog plants after they've been killed by frost, cover the roots in their containers with moist packing material (several sheets of damp newspaper, for example), and cover the containers with plastic trash bags. Then store the plants inside a garage or other protected place at temperatures of not more than 40° F, which will keep them dormant. Keep the plants moist throughout the winter, then return them to the pond after the ice has melted in the spring.　—*Nancy Beaubaire*

of water iris—*Iris fulva* (red), *Iris versicolor* (blue) and *Iris pseudacorus* (yellow). These are all planted on the 8-in.-deep ledge. We ordered three different water lilies that are hardy in Zone 8—*Nymphaea* 'Marliacea Albida' (white flowers), *Nymphaea* 'Charlene Strawn' (yellow) and *Nymphaea* 'Splendida' (red)—as well as the bog plant pickerel rush (*Pontederia cordata*) and a submerged plant, anacharis (*Elodea canadensis*). All our plants are thriving with full sun from midmorning to late afternoon, and we have a succession of bloom from early spring through the fall.

Most aquatic plants have invasive tendencies that could turn a well-ordered pond into a water jungle, and planting them in containers makes it easier to maintain and move them. Wrapped in plastic, our mail-order plants arrived as crowns with three or four leaves. We potted all but the anacharis in 11-qt. brown plastic dishpans, using our clay loam topsoil as the potting medium. (We'd been told commercial potting mixes will float out of the container.) When potting lilies, we made sure that the tops of the crowns weren't covered with soil—the growing points must be exposed. After thoroughly watering the soil, we covered it with ½ in. of well-washed pea gravel to prevent soil from floating out. As for the anacharis, we simply tossed it in the water and it has grown fine just floating around. You could plant it in a container to avoid a rampantly growing plant like ours.

The pond wasn't completed when we received the plants, so we potted and stored them in a shallow plastic swimming pool filled with water and placed under a shade tree. Later, all but the lilies went on the ledge. We set the lilies on bricks to ensure that the soil surface would be submerged under about 18 in. to 20 in. of water.

The lilies contribute more than just their flowers. After we filled the pond, a floating green algae quickly built up. (A moss-like algae also appeared on the liner, but it actually enhances the look of the pond, so we don't worry about it.) Algal spores are airborne, so its appearance was no surprise. Within about six weeks, however, the lilies and anacharis had eliminated the floating algae. The anacharis does most of the job, competing with algae for dissolved nutrients and also filtering suspended particulates; the water lilies shade the water surface, reducing the light available to the algae. Patience is advisable during this time—if you clean out the algae manually, it will return and you'll still have to wait for the anacharis to do its work. We started with a dozen bunches of anacharis, each 8 in. to 10 in. long, and three lily plants. Lilypons recommends one bunch of anacharis per 2 sq. ft. of water surface, but our combination of plants eventually eliminated the algal growth. Occasionally, we'll get an algal "bloom" after we fertilize the plants, but the water soon clears.

We stocked the pond with Japanese calico fantails (*Carassius auratus*), attractive, mild-mannered fish that grow to 6 in. to 7 in. long. As a general rule of thumb, a pond should be stocked at the rate of no more than 1 in. of fish per 3 gal. of water. We started out with only six fish, but these have spawned, and in spite of the parents' tendency to eat their young, a few of the fry have survived. We now have about 30 fish, roughly half of what the pond will support.

Maintaining the pond has been quite simple. We fertilize the water lilies monthly and the rest of the pond plants bimonthly with commercial fertilizer tablets called Lilytabs (20-10-5), pushing the recommended number of tablets into the container down to the root zone. The plants grew rapidly, and we divided them the second spring, giving away those we didn't want. We regularly net dead leaves and flowers out of the water because anaerobic bacteria can grow in this organic matter and produce gases toxic to fish. Although we don't have one, a pool vacuum would be helpful to collect the detritus that settles on the pond bottom. Every day or two, debris needs to be scraped off the outside of the pump screen. It's also a good idea to clean the impeller every couple of months—you can judge the frequency by the time of year and amount of leaves falling in the pond.

Ponds are supposed to need emptying and cleaning only every other year, but heavy rains washed soil from our unplanted berm into the pond the first spring, forcing an early cleaning. After removing the fish and plants to a plastic swimming pool, we pumped out the water and debris, and then sponged the liner with clean water before refilling. With 240 frost-free days and temperatures seldom below 15°F, we don't need to do anything special to protect the plants or fish during the winter. (See sidebar at left for cold-weather care.)

A few pitfalls accompany the irresistible attraction of water-lily ponds. Fascinated small children should be watched closely, and mischievous older children can cause problems with games such as "spearfishing." Other, more efficient predators (herons, raccoons and snakes) can threaten the fish, but fortunately we have encountered few of these. Our cats' aversion to water seems to exceed their desire to catch fish, and our two dogs have finally realized after several lectures that the pond was not built for their enjoyment.

In spite of these drawbacks, we couldn't be more pleased with our pond. The sweetest bowl of figs ever plucked from the old tree would be no match for the serene and alluring water garden that replaced it.　□

Ed Nichols farms and makes furniture in Canton, Mississippi.

A candle glows in a homemade garden lantern. The three pieces—pedestal, enclosure and roof—were cast in tinted concrete with easily-made wooden forms.

Making a Garden Lantern

Shape your own design in concrete with homemade wooden forms

by Mark Kane

The windows and overhanging roof of a garden lantern extend a welcome that graces any outdoor space. I admire the effect, but for years I saved my garden budget for plants. Finally, inspired by the example of thrifty ingenuity shown in the photo on p. 83, I made my own lantern. My backyard is small and shady, and in keeping with the hostas and ferns I'm planting, I wanted a lantern of simple design and modest size. In my mind, I saw crisp edges and flat planes, made by casting concrete in homemade wooden forms. Construction proved to be easy and fun. If

you're at all handy, you can make your own lantern, too, or other simple garden accessories such as pots and planters.

Designing the lantern

Before I set pencil to paper, I looked at books about Japanese and Chinese gardens. The lanterns on view ranged from monoliths with alcoves for candles to miniature houses on legs, with mullioned windows and dragon roofs. The monoliths aside, the lanterns had the same elements: a base—either legs or a column—topped by a capital; an enclosure to shelter a candle from the wind; a broad roof to break the rain; and a finial atop the roof.

My design looks traditional, but keeps construction simple. I made the roof a shallow pyramid with its tip cut off (and

no finial) so the form would be basically four triangles. I chose to make a pedestal rather than a base with legs so I could build the form with a few rectangular pieces. The enclosure is more complicated, with four windows and a reveal on the bottom for a shadow line, but the forms were still simple shapes.

To size the pieces, I sketched a side view of the lantern on graph paper, erasing and redrawing lines until the proportions looked right. Then I cut the pieces out of paper, full-scale, to check the dimensions. After repeating the cycle twice, I had the sizes I wanted: an 18-in.-high pedestal, which I would set so 8 in. remained above ground; a 7-in.-square enclosure; and a 12-in.-square roof, sloped at 20°.

You can easily resize my design to fit your needs, modify the pieces or come up with a new design altogether. You might like ornamentation, which I scanted. I was content with a recess on each face of the pedestal, a bevel on the underside of the capital, and flared windows so light can spill out at wide angles. You could get fancier: add beveled corners, trace geometric patterns on the molds with glue or caulk, or attach leaves, flowers and twigs to the molds. I planned the lantern to use candles, but you can make a raceway for electric wires by setting a length of ½-in. pipe in the center of the pedestal form, with an elbow leading out to one side at the bottom.

Constructing the lantern

Concrete forms have to come apart easily and cleanly, without fracturing the concrete. I made the lantern forms from 1×2s, 1×3s, and ¼-in. plywood, with many of the plywood pieces cut at 45° angles on the edges so I could pull each one off without disturbing its neighbors. The exceptions were the plywood pieces in the center of the enclosure. They were cut at 90°, set in place, and braced with the 1×3 shown in the drawing. To disassemble them, I pulled the 1×3 and then the plywood pieces. The window flare helps disassembly, too—it lets the forms pull out cleanly. I used duct tape and drywall screws to assemble the forms so I could unfasten the pieces without stressing the concrete or ruining the forms. It took about three hours to make the forms, and, with care, I can reuse them many times.

I darkened the concrete, because I thought its natural pale gray would be obtrusive in the garden. Concrete colors are dry pigments, sold by suppliers who serve masons. I chose black, and bought the smallest quantity available—5 lb. (for $12). Other pigments include red, brown and green. Experiment before you cast the lantern. The color barely changed when I stirred the pigment into dry ready-mix concrete, but it darkened dramatically when I added water, and then lightened as the concrete cured. After a few test batches, I settled on a pigment/concrete ratio of 1:10, which produced dark-gray concrete.

Casting the lantern pieces takes a little patience. Resist the temptation to over-wet the concrete so you can pour it into the forms. For strength, you want a fairly stiff mix—just wet enough to be sticky. Concrete adheres to wood, so paint the forms with motor oil before you cast the lantern pieces. I filled the forms a few inches at a time, tamping and churning each layer with a thin stick to eliminate air pockets and to drive the concrete into all the corners. When the forms were full, I tapped them all over with a hammer. Tapping has the same effect as smoothing wet concrete with a trowel: it displaces rocks and pebbles, leaving sand at the surface. If you want a lantern with smooth faces, tap the forms thoroughly.

As soon as you've cast the pieces, set the forms where they won't be disturbed and leave them there at least a week. Concrete develops strength by "curing"—a process of chemical bonding that proceeds rapidly during the first week or so, and continues more slowly for weeks, or months. Disassemble the forms as gently as possible, and handle the fresh concrete with care. If it's still wet, the corners will be soft and easily nicked, and the thinner pieces can crack under mild stress. Before you set up the lantern in the garden, let the pieces air-cure until they're dry on the surface. I got eager and pulled the enclosure forms after three days, which was too early—the concrete cracked. I let the pieces dry and put them back together with epoxy glue. Though the repair was sturdy, the cracks showed, so I reassembled the forms and cast another enclosure. After curing a week, the concrete remained intact when I pulled the forms.

Installing the lantern takes ten minutes. I dug a hole with a posthole digger and lowered the pedestal into it. As I tamped dirt around the pedestal, I checked the capital with a hand level to make sure it was horizontal. Then I set the enclosure on the capital and gently set the roof in place. As I hoped, the roof is heavy enough (about 15 lb.) to endure strong winds without lifting off.

I'm pleased with the lantern. The price was right—around $30 for materials. The design is nicely proportioned and the size is appropriate for the yard. The only formal element in sight, the lantern lends my gawky young garden an air of dignity. At dusk, with a candle glowing in the windows, it seems to watch over the garden and its maker. □

Mark Kane is an associate editor at Fine Gardening *magazine.*

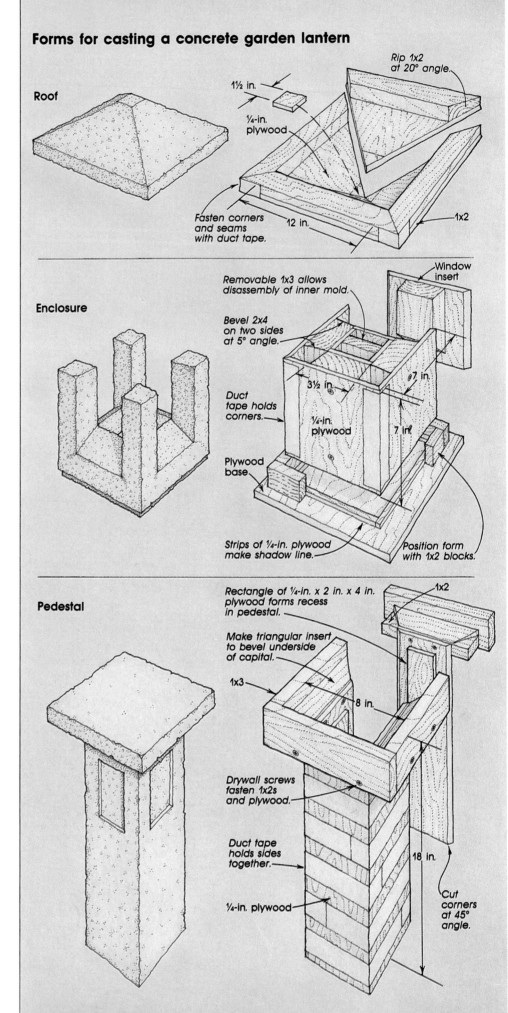

Forms for casting a concrete garden lantern

Roof

Rip 1x2 at 20° angle.

1½ in.

¼-in. plywood

Fasten corners and seams with duct tape.

12 in.

1x2

Enclosure

Window insert

Removable 1x3 allows disassembly of inner mold.

Bevel 2x4 on two sides at 5° angle.

3½ in.

7 in.

Duct tape holds corners.

¼-in. plywood

7 in.

Plywood base

Strips of ¼-in. plywood make shadow line.

Position form with 1x2 blocks.

Pedestal

Rectangle of ¼-in. x 2 in. x 4 in. plywood forms recess in pedestal.

1x2

Make triangular insert to bevel underside of capital.

1x3

8 in.

Drywall screws fasten 1x2s and plywood.

Duct tape holds sides together.

¼-in. plywood

18 in.

Cut corners at 45° angle.

Household objects make a garden lantern

by Ann Stacey

Among the utensils in your kitchen, the miscellaneous scraps in your workshop and the supplies in your garden shed, you probably have the ingredients for casting a concrete garden lantern. I did. With an assortment of "off-the-shelf" objects, I made the lantern shown here. All you need are a bit of imagination and an inquiring eye.

What triggered the urge to brighten one little corner of my garden with a Japanese-style "stone" lantern was finding a bag of cement at a garage sale. The price was irresistible. My husband warned me that old cement is no bargain, but by then I was firmly in an experimental mood.

What could I use for molds? I sketched a number of lantern designs, and then simplified, simplified, simplified. My old graniteware bread-dough bowl looked like a good shape for the base of the lantern. I

Brightening a corner amid conifers, this concrete lantern was cast in forms made from a bread bowl and lid, two nursery pots, and a plastic bottle.

figured that concrete wouldn't stick to it—it still felt oily from those days when I was baking some 30 loaves of bread per week for my six teenagers. The wide lid looked suitable for the lantern's roof. Two plastic nursery pots, one about 4 in. wider than the other, would do for the middle, and a plastic 2-liter soda bottle would be perfect for the knob on top. To make windows in the middle and arches in the base, I cut appropriate shapes from a 2-in.-thick sheet of polystyrene insulation, the white beady stuff that you can saw with a bread knife. To round out my supplies, I collected a few plastic bags and leather gloves. The bags would keep concrete from sticking to the molds, and the gloves would protect my skin as I patted the concrete into place. (Wet concrete is alkaline enough to dry and crack skin after prolonged handling.)

I mixed up a stiff batch of concrete in a wheelbarrow, with one part cement, two parts sand, four parts gravel, and only enough water to dampen everything completely while leaving the mix dry-looking and crumbly. Making concrete is a lot like mixing piecrust dough: too much water ruins the recipe.

First, I shaped the base of the lantern. I taped four Styrofoam arches inside the bread bowl and then pressed concrete into the bowl with my gloved hands. I shaped the concrete about 3 in. thick at the bottom of the bowl and a little more than 2 in. thick at the top.

For the roof of the lantern, I lined the lid of the bread bowl with a piece of plastic bag and then pressed concrete into the lid roughly 2 in. thick, firming and shaping the edges by hand.

For the middle, I lined the larger nursery pot with a plastic bag and tamped 2 in. of concrete in the bottom. Next I slipped the smaller pot into a plastic bag and set the pot on top of the concrete. Then I firmed 3 in. of concrete into the ring-shaped space between the two pots, set the polystyrene windows in place and finished filling the mold. I tamped the concrete with a stick to make sure no air pockets persisted, and I smoothed the top with a trowel.

I finished the job by stopping the mouth of a cut-off soda bottle with a pebble and tamping concrete into the bottle, and then I set all the various pieces of my lantern in the garage and covered them with an old blanket. I sprinkled water on the blanket several times over the next few days to keep the concrete from drying too quickly. When I turned the pieces out of the molds after three days, I'm pleased to say that they looked better than I'd expected. I pulled the polystyrene pieces out of the windows and arches, trimmed up the openings with a knife, and was done.

Assembled in the garden, the lantern isn't the least bit wobbly, even when the cats climb over the top. I painted the concrete with buttermilk in the hope that moss will get started on it and lend a bit of false antiquity. And I still have enough cement left over for another project. Maybe a birdbath? □

Ann Stacey gardens in East Selkirk, Manitoba.

Casting a concrete garden lantern with off-the-shelf forms

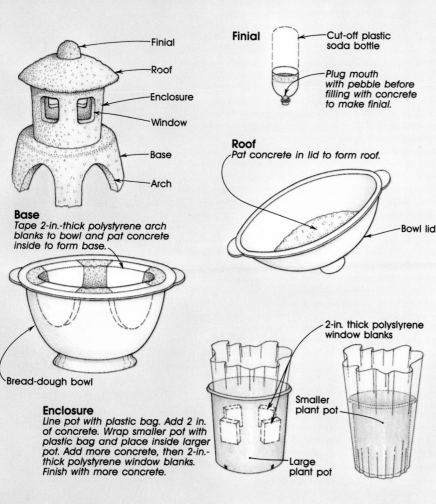

Finial

Roof

Enclosure

Window

Base

Arch

Base
Tape 2-in.-thick polystyrene arch blanks to bowl and pat concrete inside to form base.

Bread-dough bowl

Enclosure
Line pot with plastic bag. Add 2 in. of concrete. Wrap smaller pot with plastic bag and place inside larger pot. Add more concrete, then 2-in.-thick polystyrene window blanks. Finish with more concrete.

Finial

Cut-off plastic soda bottle

Plug mouth with pebble before filling with concrete to make finial.

Roof
Pat concrete in lid to form roof.

Bowl lid

2-in. thick polystyrene window blanks

Smaller plant pot

Large plant pot

Photo: Ann Stacey; illustration: Vince Babak

Since installing this fence, the author hasn't had a single deer visit her garden. Here, an open gate with wings bends sharply to bar deer.

The Ultimate Deer Fence

Electronics and design innovations make this fence 100% effective

by Molly Hackett

Ten years ago when I first planted my garden, I had flowers, vegetables and deer—not a workable combination. I watched deer walk daintily across my garden beds, picking at a variety of vegetables and uprooting those they didn't fancy.

I tried every deer deterrent I could find, commercial and homemade, without much success. When deer ate my 6-in. high peas during the lushest spring in memory, I knew that the time had come for a permanent deer deterrent—a fence. I finally settled on a design that has kept my garden free of deer since I put it in two years ago.

Planning the fence

First I did research. I thought about the site and what the fence needed to accomplish. I wanted it to be effective; I wanted parts of it to be almost in-

visible, and I wanted the visible parts to be reasonably attractive. I planned to use existing plantings to screen the fence, and to add native plants, which are more deer-resistant and weather-resistant, along the outside. I talked to the local game warden and looked at the big-game fence around a nearby commercial orchard. Then I drew a rough plan of a deer fence that would enclose only the irrigated acre surrounding our house.

To keep the fenced area from looking boxed-in, I designed the fence with only one 90° corner. The other corners had wider angles. I wanted pressure-treated, wooden posts and braces at the corners and at the gates, and metal fence posts in between. The heavy wooden posts that hold the weight of the fence would be fairly visible, but I felt they would harmonize well with the mountain scenery; the metal fence posts would be less visible. I planned to install wire fencing 6 ft. high, with room at the top of the posts to add another foot or two of wire in case a world-

class jumper should ever migrate into the neighborhood.

I decided to install a traditional gate in the center of each length of fence, on the principle that there can't be too many gates. At two corners I installed special deer-proof gates that consist of wings on either side of a narrow, 20-in. opening, allowing people to enter, while excluding deer. (See illustration above.) Finally, where the driveway meets the fence, I planned an open gate with an alarm system. This gate is monitored by an electronic eye that triggers flood lights and a beeper, scaring intruders away.

The length of the deer fence totaled 600 ft., and the cost came to about $1.65 per running foot, with about $80 going for materials for the electronic sensing device. For the corners we bought 8-in. diameter posts in 10-ft. lengths. The braces and the poles for the V-gates were 4-in. diameter wooden rails. We found 8-ft. steel posts with T-shaped cross sections for the rest of the fence. We could not find 6-ft. wide wire fencing, so we used

Photos: Ellyn P. Jones

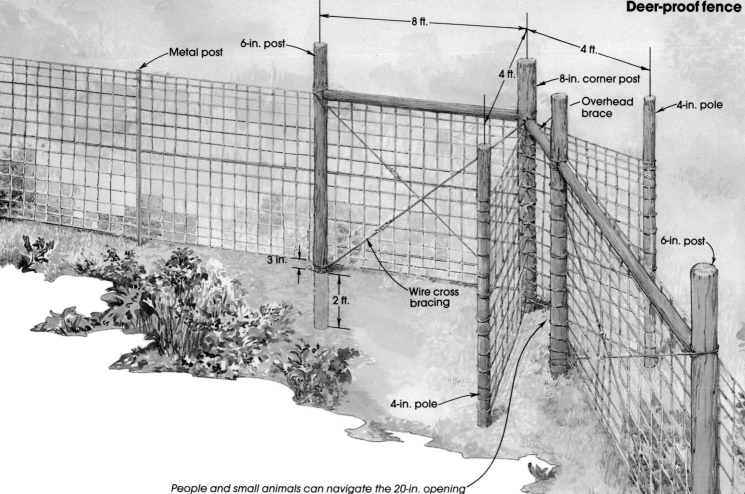

Metal post

6-in. post

8 ft.

4 ft.

4 ft.

8-in. corner post

Overhead brace

4-in. pole

6-in. post

3 in.

2 ft.

Wire cross bracing

4-in. pole

People and small animals can navigate the 20-in. opening and sharp turn of this gate, but deer can't.

one width each of 39-in. and 32-in. fencing, for an effective height of just under 6 ft.

Building the fence

The actual construction of the fence went very smoothly, thanks to prior planning. It took five of us a week, working in our spare time, but a fence like this could be built by two people in one weekend.

We started by setting posts along the fence line, using a power auger (available at equipment rental stores) to dig the holes. We used a metal fence post as a ruler to measure the 8-ft. spacing between posts, and made minor adjustments in gate and corners for even spacing. Where possible, we ran the fence so that a deer would look uphill toward it, for an illusion of even greater height.

The wooden posts that the gates hang from in the center of each length of fence have to resist the pull of that entire side of the fence, so we put a horizontal brace between the posts above each gate. The brace acts as

a stretcher, keeping the vertical posts from leaning. We braced the three wooden support posts at corners in the same way. Since the corner posts and braces have to withstand the pull of taut fence wire, we strengthened them with crisscrossing diagonal wires between the posts. When all the posts were set, we were ready to stretch the wire fencing. We used the 39-in. wide fencing on the bottom and the 32-in. wide fencing on top. For the sake of appearance, we put the lower width of fencing upside down. The bottoms of both sections meet in the center, with the large holes at eye level.

We rolled the fencing out and stapled it to the first corner with heavy fence staples on every other horizontal wire. Then we stretched the wire to the next corner, using a homemade fence stretcher made from two 2×4s the width of the fencing. (The fencing was sandwiched between the 2×4s.) We pulled the wire until it was just taut.

As we stretched each section, we stapled the wire to the posts. Where each section ended at a gate, we first

stapled, then wrapped the wire around the post and fastened it to itself. We kept the bottom of the wire about 3 in. above the ground to maximize the height of the fence and ensure that the lowest wire wouldn't be buried in the ground within a few years.

When we'd made the entire round, we went back and attached the fencing to the metal posts with special fence clips. Then we attached the two widths of fencing to each other with hog rings, which are available at farm supply and hardware stores. Finally, we painted the tops of the metal posts (which are always manufactured with a contrasting color for visibility) to match the bottoms.

Innovative gates mean success

Gates we had seen along a Colorado

Light-and-buzzer deer security system

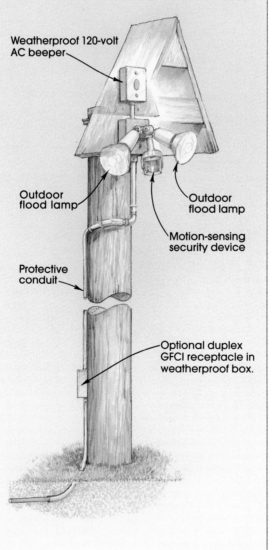

The author's gateless driveway is monitored by a standard motion-sensing security light. The motion detector triggers lights and a beeper around the clock to frighten deer. This unusual security system is housed in a birdhouse-like box attached to a fence post at the driveway entrance.

A standard motion-sensing security light with one modification constitutes an effective deer deterrent. Used to frighten deer away from an open gate, it could also protect other areas, such as a flower border, up to a radius of 70 ft. A built-in sensing device turns on the lights. The modification is a beeper that sounds when the lights turn on. The sensor ordinarily turns itself on at dusk and off at dawn. To make it run day and night, the author turns its switch to the test position.

You can do the installation yourself, if you're handy, or get an electrician to wire the beeper into the security light and install the system. Select a unit that is easy to open for rewiring, and be sure to comply with state and local electrical codes.

To install the system, mount a weatherproof beeper in a junction box with a hole in the cover to expose the beeper. Wire the beeper into the security light, connecting its black wire to the black wires in the security light, and its white wire to the white wires in the security light. Secure both connections with wire nuts. Mount the unit about 8 ft. high on a fence post. Run 12/2 underground cable with ground wire from the lighting unit through conduit down the pole and underground to a GFCI-protected receptacle or circuit breaker. Tightly seal all joints in the conduit and between conduit and junction boxes with silicone caulk. Make sure all hardware is well grounded.

—Delilah Smittle

Weatherproof 120-volt AC beeper

Outdoor flood lamp

Outdoor flood lamp

Motion-sensing security device

Protective conduit

Optional duplex GFCI receptacle in weatherproof box.

interstate highway inspired the V-shaped walk-through gates that we installed at two of the fence corners. The gates are simply a 20-in. wide break in the fence, with two 4-ft. long sections of fence that project like wings on either side of the opening, forming an angle to walk through. (See illustration on previous page.) We worked out the size of the opening and the angle of the wings experimentally on the ground before constructing the gate. The fencing on each wing is stapled to the corner post and to a 4-in. diameter pole set vertically into the ground.

The driveway to the house has no gate, although the posts are set 16 ft. apart to hold a standard-sized gate, should we ever need it. Instead of a gate, we installed a motion sensor which activates two security lights and an attached beeper. The motion-sensing security light, which costs about $20, is a common security light unit. The beeper, also about $20, is the type typically used to alert people to turn off home security systems, such as the Sonalert model SC110P made by Mallory (available at electronic supply stores). (See "Light-and-buzzer deer security system" at left.)

The sensor, set to provide 15 seconds of light and noise whenever it is activated, has proven 100% effective. For a month, the deer set it off at all hours. Since then, they have circled just outside the area where they would trigger the sensor.

So far, the fence has needed no maintenance. I will need to renew the stain I put on the wooden posts and gates from time to time, but the treated wood should last up to 30 years. The first beeper had to be replaced within a year. Otherwise, the electronic sentry has performed flawlessly.

Inside the fence, our garden produces flowers, fruits and vegetables in abundance. The only disadvantage I have found is that the sensor can be set off by large flying insects. I sometimes turn it off rather than listen to the frequent beeps as I work in the garden.

The fence has been a wonderful solution. We still watch the deer, but without the clutch of fear we used to feel. The deer seem confident that they will not be bothered outside the fence; they feed and play where we can watch such spectacles as the growth of antlers on a four-point buck. □

Molly Hackett gardens in Victor, Montana.

Growing and Crafting Gourds

Vigorous vines yield useful and decorative fruit

Gourds come in all different shapes and sizes. The collection above includes a strangely contoured maranka (far left), a portly wine kettle (center), a mini bottle (front center) and two long-handled dippers (far right). The woody shells can persist indefinitely, making gourds excellent raw material for crafts and utensils.

by Mary Ann Rood

Gourds have been part of my gardens ever since I graduated from growing radishes in my sandbox. I like the surprises these plants give. A rambunctious gourd vine might grow right up a pine tree and produce yard-long fruit shaped like a caveman's club. And when frost kills the rioting vines that stay on the ground, I discover giant, green pumpkin shapes, twisting gourd snakes or brightly colored, warty pears. Best of all, when winter descends, leaving other gar-

Gourd (*Luffa* spp., *Cucurbita pepo* var. *ovifera, Lagenaria siceraria*)

- Vigorous annual vine closely related to squashes, pumpkins and melons. Grown for its ornamental and useful fruit.

- Yellow or white flowers, depending on species.

- Fruits mature in 90 to 120 or more days depending on species and growing conditions.

- Requires full sun, soil rich in organic matter and copious amounts of water.

- Fruits of many varieties used for craft and utensil making.

deners to daydream over seed catalogs, I turn my harvest into an incredible array of things—sensible and silly, decorative and useful.

Gourds are really squash with ambition. Like squash, gourds belong to the *Cucurbitaceae* family, which also includes cucumbers and melons. And, like others in this family, many gourds are edible. But gourds can be much more. Their durable shells can be cut, carved and painted for myriad uses—everything from cups and bowls to elaborate decorative items.

Gourds have been associated with humankind since before we dug our first gardens outside our caves. Wild gourds served as kitchenware for Mesolithic cooks. Native Americans,

Photo: Susan Kahn; illustration, Rosalind Loeb Wanke

who made extensive use of gourds, passed on many of their traditions to the early colonists. Today gourds serve mainly to delight. Nearly 4,000 modern gourd lovers belong to The American Gourd Society (see Resources at right). Chapters across the country celebrate the partnership of gourds and gardeners with festivals featuring competitions for gourd size and shape, and exhibitions of gourd crafts ranging from carved vases and lamps to dolls and jewelry.

Types of gourds

The gourds most commonly grown in the United States fall into three main categories. The most unusual, to those who have only passing knowledge of gourds, are the luffa or sponge gourds (*Luffa* spp.). That a luffa, the familiar backscrubber, is a gourd or a plant at all surprises many people. Luffa fruits, which grow 12 in. to 24 in. long, need only to be dried and peeled to be your best friend in the bathtub. They also serve as excellent scrubbers for Teflon® pans. You can even cook young luffas like zucchini or okra.

More familiar are the ornamentals, small, brightly colored gourds seen on porches and dinner tables in the fall. These yellow-flowered gourds are known botanically as *Cucurbita pepo* var. *ovifera*. Their common names usually describe their shapes: spoon, orange, apple, egg. Fresh, ornamentals decorate harvest tables; dried, they can be made into decorative crafts such as Christmas ornaments.

My favorite type is the hardshell gourd (*Lagenaria siceraria*). The thick, durable skins of these gourds are ideal for making utensils or crafts, as people long ago discovered. And they come in a huge variety of shapes and sizes. The night-opening, white flowers of this gourd plant eventually yield fruits that vary in size from the 3-in.-tall miniature bottles to the mammoth African wine kettles, which measure as much as 88 in. around and often weigh more than 100 lbs. The names we use for hardshell gourds often reflect the uses to which our great-grandmothers put them: dippers, sugar troughs, birdhouses. Before tin cans and Tupperware® usurped their place in American households, these gourds served a multitude of uses.

Growing gourds

Growing gourds is very much like growing pumpkins or squashes. Give them rich, well-drained soil improved with lots of organic matter, plenty of water and a sunny location. Gourds haven't even heard about bush habit, so give them room. I space ornamental gourds 3 ft. apart in rows 4 ft. apart.

Gourd vines, like those of melons, squashes and pumpkins, grow with abandon when given full sun, humus-rich soil and lots of water. Here, a dipper gourd hangs from an overrun fence.

RESOURCES

The largest selection of gourd seeds in the United States is available through **The American Gourd Society**, P.O. Box 274, Mt. Gilead, OH 43338-0274. The Society also publishes a quarterly magazine, sells books and holds an annual convention. Dues are $5 per year.

The author recommends the following seed companies. They offer a selection of named varieties.

Meta Horticultural Labs, Meta, KY 41501, 606-432-1516. Catalog free.

Native Seeds/SEARCH, 2509 N. Campbell Ave. #325, Tucson, AZ 85719. Catalog $1.00. Specializes in gourds grown in the Southwest.

Nichols Garden Nursery, 1190 North Pacific Highway, Albany, OR 97321, 503-928-9280. Catalog free.

Stokes Seeds, Box 548, Buffalo, NY 14240, 416-688-4300. Catalog free.

You can also save your own seeds from the gourds you grow. Be aware that varieties within a species readily cross-pollinate. Unless you grow just one variety, you will get unpredictable results.

Luffas and hardshells require even more space. I plant those at least 4 ft. apart in rows 6 ft. apart.

When to sow your seeds depends on the length of your growing season and on the gourd variety you are growing. You can plant the seeds of ornamentals directly in the garden once the danger of frost has passed. They mature about 90 days from planting, so to determine when to sow, I count backward from the time when I want the colors to be at their best. Hardshells need more time, usually 100 to 110 days; the longer the growing season, the thicker and more durable the shell. Luffas require the longest season of all—upwards of 120 days. Gardeners with short growing seasons may want to consider starting plants indoors. Since gourds resent having their roots disturbed, start seeds in large peat pots to minimize transplant shock.

You can let your gourd vines ramble around on the ground or you can train them up some sort of trellis or even a tree. Trellising allows you to grow more plants in a given space. Keep in mind that the larger hardshells can get very heavy; anything bigger than a birdhouse gourd will pull itself off the vine. I usually save trellis space for dipper and spoon gourds. Their "handles" grow straight, rather than curving, if the vines are elevated off the ground.

Harvesting and curing

The key to harvesting gourds is not to pick them before they are mature. If harvested too early, gourds of all kinds rot rather than cure, or dry. Because hardshells and luffas require a fairly long growing season, the arrival of frost signals harvesting time for these gourds in most areas of the country. In warmer climates, harvest hardshells when the vine begins to turn brown where it meets the gourd; luffas are ready when the fruits are dark brown and nearly dried out inside. The shorter-season ornamental gourds have no such clear indicator of maturity. My favorite clue is the squeeze play. Starting with the youngest gourds (at the end of the vine), I gently squeeze the developing fruit, working my way toward the hill. When I feel a gourd that is "set," not squishy, I harvest it, along with the gourds nearer the hill, which are older and certain to be mature. For all gourds, cut—don't pull—the fruit from the vine and leave an inch or two of stem attached.

After harvesting, wash the gourds

Photo: Thomas E. Eltzroth

with either a Borax® solution (available at your local supermarket) or with a mild solution of chlorine bleach, and store all but the ornamentals in a dry, airy place. Have patience. Gourds are more than 90% water. The gradual evaporation of this water is the curing process. Depending on the size of the gourd and the storage conditions, curing may take anywhere from three weeks to six months.

Meanwhile, you can coat ornamentals with liquid floor wax (varnish or shellac will encourage rot in uncured ornamentals), and use them for table decorations. When their early career in the spotlight is over, and their colors begin to fade, put them with their curing comrades in the attic or barn.

Gourds have two skins, a thin, membranous outer one and a thick, woody one underneath. The color in ornamentals is in the outer layer and cannot be effectively preserved. In both hardshells and ornamentals, this outer skin can shrivel and mold during the curing process. The gourd isn't actually rotting; it's just going through its awkward age. As long as the woody shell remains hard, keep waiting. If a gourd turns black, gets soft and collapses, however, that's real rot—usually the result of too-early harvesting or of bruising. Throw such gourds out.

The fungus on the outer skin leaves a mottled pattern on the shell underneath. Some people find this attractive; others find it disfiguring. If you want a smooth, evenly tan surface (for later burning or painting, for example), you can scrape the outer skin away and wash the gourd about once a week with a disinfectant to keep fungi at bay until the gourd has cured. To remove the outer skin, let the gourd dry for a week or so after harvesting; then pull a paring knife across the surface. If a bead of water forms be-

hind it, wait another week. Then, scrape carefully with a paring knife, fine steel wool or a wire brush.

Treat luffas a bit differently. Hang them to dry to reduce the chance of rotting. If the seeds rattle when you move the gourd, shake them out through the small flap at one end that readily pops out when dry, and soak the luffa to soften the skin before peeling. Bleaching will even out most discolorations and whiten the sponge.

Getting a start on gourd craft

When the seeds inside rattle, ornamental and hardshell gourds are ready to be turned into whatever your imag-

The craft potential of gourds is unlimited. The owner of this gourd carved the hard outer layer and dyed the corky inner layer to reveal characters suggested by "The Twelve Days of Christmas."

ination suggests. If you plan to paint, varnish or shellac the gourd, start by scrubbing off the outer skin with steel wool or copper pot scrubbers. Sanding with increasingly fine sandpapers and steel wool produces a glassy, glossy finish for burning or fine painting.

Treat gourds like wood. You can saw, drill, carve, burn with a woodburning tool, paint, stain or wax them. The possiblities are endless, and so is the variety of the tools you can use. Craft knives and woodcarving sets are handy for cutting and carving, as are such improvised tools as nails embedded in dowel handles or screwdrivers sharpened on concrete. You can engrave gourds with a thick needle, like the specialty needles available in sewing stores, or with an embroidery needle broken in half and stuck in a pencil eraser. Woodburning kits found in toy stores or crafts supply stores can be used to beautiful effect on gourds, especially when combined with wood stains for shading.

Many crafters are unaccustomed to working with a curved surface. Graph paper helps in planning designs. To transfer the design to the gourd, put carbon paper behind the completed design and trace it. Rubber bands stretched around the gourd aid in the drawing of guidelines.

Another way gourds are unusual is that the woody shell itself has two layers—a brown, hard outer layer and a cream-colored, corky underlayer. Carving through the outer surface reveals the lighter-colored inner layer, resulting in an attractive contrast. If you then apply wood stain or a fabric or leather dye to the gourd, the porous underlayer will soak up more color than the outer layer, turning darker. Carve into the dyed inner layer and you again expose light-colored areas, thereby achieving three contrasts.

Gourd craft is very accessible. You can share its pleasures with children and with older people, who may tell you about drinking from gourd dippers at their grandparents' well or how eggs stored in a gourd won't spoil. You can make practical things like birdhouses and sewing boxes. You can even make gourd Garfield the Cats. When you do, you'll join a tradition older than history. □

Mary Ann Rood gardens and writes in Apex, North Carolina. She is the third- generation president of the Gourd Village Garden Club in Cary, North Carolina.

From moldy basketball gourd to grinning jack-o'-lantern: begin the transformation by cleaning away the dried outer skin, then trace and cut. Finally, paint the inside to enrich the light of a small flashlight; a real candle would send the woody gourd up in flames.

Photos: top, Raymond Konan; below, Susan Kahn

Forcing Bulbs
Cold tricks them into winter bloom

VIDEO TAKES
SEE PAGE 93

A gallery of forced spring bulbs paints a windowsill with color. The brown bells of fritillary bloom in the foreground; behind them are daffodils (left) and a pot of tulips with a skirt of golden crocuses (right).

by Mark Kane

Last December, my house had an early spring. While snow fell outside, the long bay window in the dining room bloomed with spring flowers.

Grape hyacinths raised their blue spikes; daffodils assembled in white and yellow drifts; tiny miniature irises with blue petals and yellow throats crowded together in 4-in. pots. When I came downstairs in the morning, the welcome smell of flowers met my nose and the sight of sunlit colors made the start of the gardening year seem just a little bit closer.

I owed my wintertime harvest of color and fragrance to forcing, an old trick that fools bulbs into blooming early. Forcing is an easy thing to do. You will need potting mix, pots and a spot that will stay reliably cold but not freezing, from late fall onward. And you need some hardy, spring-flowering bulbs, such as crocuses, hyacinths, scillas, tulips and

All photos, except where noted: Susan Kahn;
above, Courtesy International Bloembollen Centrum

daffodils. (For more choices, see the chart below.) But before I tell you how to force bulbs, let me explain why forcing works.

What happens when you force bulbs

The bulbs that are suited to forcing have a topsy-turvy cycle of growth in nature and in the garden. Most of them flower early in spring, while trees are still bare. Their leaves and roots persist just long enough—through mid- to late spring—for the bulbs to store a new supply of energy. Then the leaves and roots die and the bulbs, safe underground, go dormant for the summer and part of the fall.

In fall, when the soil cools, the bulbs awaken and send out new roots, the first step in their preparation for the next spring. The roots continue to grow until the soil cools to 40°F. In most of the U.S., the bulbs produce a dense mat of roots before winter sets in. In cold climates, freezing temperatures halt the roots' growth, but they won't kill them; in warmer climates, the bulbs may keep making roots throughout the whole winter.

When spring temperatures rise into the 40's and 50's, bulbs reawaken, send up leaves, then make flowers. This growth is rapid, thanks to the full complement of roots, so leaves have plenty of time before they decline to replenish the energy of the bulbs. Then the bulbs go dormant again until fall.

Forcing exploits this cycle. In fall, you buy dormant bulbs, pot them and keep them cold for several months to stimulate them to make roots. Once plants have roots, you bring the pots to a windowsill, where the warmth persuades the bulbs that spring has arrived. In short order, they flower, and you have an early spring.

How to start forcing bulbs

The first step in forcing is to buy bulbs in fall, about six weeks before hard freezes are due. In much of the U.S., the right time comes sometime in September. Garden centers offer a selection then that includes the mainstays of the spring garden. Look for bulbs that are firm, free of mold and uniform in size. From mail-order specialists (see Sources on p. 92), you can order not only the mainstays, but also lesser-known bulbs. Prices are modest—about 10 cents to 50 cents a bulb.

Next, gather up pots in which to plant your bulbs. Almost any pot will do, provided there's enough room for roots. Pots with drainage holes and saucers are safest because they make it hard to drown roots. You can also use pots with no drainage holes, but you must water these pots with a light hand to avoid a lake in the bottom.

Use ordinary potting mix. It provides air spaces and a considerable capacity to retain moisture. You can buy it ready-made or mix your own. My recipe is 1 part shredded peat moss and 1 part perlite (small, light beads of volcanic glass). For top-heavy bulbs like daffodils planted in light plastic containers, add ¼ part sand; the extra weight helps anchor the containers.

When you plant the bulbs, put them high in the pot and space them closely. Fill a pot ¾ full with potting mix. Set the bulbs close together on top of the mix, and then add more mix to cover them. Most bulbs for forcing are so small—under ¾ in. in diameter—that you can space them less than 1 in. apart. Close spacing looks good. A dozen grape hyacinths in a 6-in. pot make a good strong show of color, and the crowding doesn't bother them. The exceptions are daffodils and paperwhites; both need about 1 in. to 2 in. of space between bulbs.

I like to grow small bulbs such as crocuses or grape hyacinths in 4 in. pots. Then I can gather five or six pots at a time on the windowsill in any combination I please—all grape hyacinths to make a single sweep of color or a mix of bulbs for variety. You can get the same effects in larger pots by

Bulbs and times for forcing
Here are 17 bulbs that can be forced for winter bloom:

Common name (Botanical name)	Weeks of cold	Weeks to bloom
Crocus (Crocus chysanthus)	15	2-3
Crocus (Crocus vernus)	15	2
Daffodils (Narcissus)	15-17	2-3
Fritillary (Fritillaria meleagris)	15	3
Glory of the snow (Chionodoxa luciliae)	15	2-3
Grape hyacinth (Muscari armeniacum)	13-15	2-3
Grape hyacinth (Muscari botryoides alba)	14-15	2-3
Hyacinth (Hyacinthus)	11-14	2-3
Iris (Iris danfordiae)	15	2-3
Iris (Iris reticulata)	15	2-3
Paperwhites (Narcissus tazetta)	none	3-5
Puschkinia (Puschkinia libanotica)	15	2-3
Scilla (Scilla siberica)	15	2-3
Scilla (Scilla tubergeniana)	12-15	2-3
Snowdrop (Galanthus nivalis)	15	2
Tulip (Tulipa)	14-20	2-3
Winter aconite (Eranthis hyemalis)	15	2

A parade of bulbs
Bulbs for forcing vary in shape and size. Shoots grow from the top; roots from the bottom. Plant bottom-end-down.

Top
Bottom
Emerging new shoot

Daffodil   Puschkinia   Grape hyacinth   Dwarf iris   Crocus   Glory of the snow   Scilla

How to force bulbs

Into the pot

Close spacing

Into the pot. To force bulbs for winter bloom, start in fall by setting dormant bulbs, with the root end down and shoot end up, into a container ¾ full of potting mix (left). The bulbs shown here are grape hyacinths. **Close spacing.** Seven bulbs fill a pot that's 6 in. in diameter (above). Close spacing yields a dramatic show of flowers. Potting mix partially covers the bulbs in the second pot, making it ready for chilling.

planting them full with one kind of bulb or by mixing several kinds together. It's tricky to mix bulbs because they may flower at different times, but you might as well experiment—you'll still have flowers, and you'll learn what works.

The right kind of cold

Once you pot your bulbs, you have to keep them cold and moist. They need three or more months of cold, dark, humid conditions to make roots. (Paperwhites are exceptions. They don't require chilling and are ready to grow and flower as soon as you pot them and set them on the windowsill.)

The simplest way to chill bulbs is to store them in your refrigerator. The temperature on the shelves is about 40°F, suitable for root growth, but refrigerators are as dry as deserts, so water the pots well, put them in plastic bags, and tie the tops of the bags to keep the mix moist. Check the pots once a month and water as needed.

If you don't want to use up your refrigerator space with pots of bulbs, there are other methods of chilling. Bulbs can be carefully buried in dry straw or leaves outdoors, placed into a cold frame, or stored on cellar stairs.

If you want to insulate your bulbs with leaves, first, pot them. Then gather up a supply of dry leaves and heap them up into a fluffy pile with plenty of air spaces. Next, choose a sheltered spot, safe from the northerly winds of winter—against your house, in the corner between your garage and compost

SOURCES

These mail-order specialists offer a wide selection of bulbs, many for forcing.

Daffodil Mart, Rte. 3, Box 794, Gloucester, VA 23061, 804-693-3966. Minimum order, $25.

Dutch Gardens, P.O. Box 200, Adelphia, N.J., 07710, 908-780-2713. Ships until Sept. 25 to North, Oct. 15 to South.

McClure & Zimmerman, 108 W. Winnebago, P.O. Box 368, Friesland, WI, 53935, 414-326-4220. Ships until Nov.

John Scheepers, P.O. Box 700, Bantam, CT 06750, 203-567-0838. Minimum order, $25. Ships through December.

Van Bourgondien, P.O. Box 1000, Babylon, NY 11702-0598, 800-622-9997. Ships through December.

pile or next to a board fence, perhaps. Arrange your containers there in a tight circle. You can stack a second, smaller circle on top of the first. Now rake up your dry leaves and heap them 1 ft. deep over the containers. Spread them at least 1 ft. beyond the circle of containers, then lightly drape a sheet of plastic or a tarp over the pile of leaves to keep them dry and anchor the edges with bricks, stones or 2×4's. Insulated by the leaves, your containers will stay cold but not frozen. To check their progress, just lift one edge of the tarp, reach through the leaves and pull out a container.

You can also chill your containers in a cold frame, but only if you're sure the cold frame stays cold. On a sunny day in early winter, even if the outside temperature is well below freezing, a cold frame can heat up to 60°F or 70°F. This heat could prompt the bulbs to start making leaves and flowers. Keep the temperature inside the cold frame low by opening the top in the morning; close it again in the late afternoon to keep temperatures from dropping below freezing. And be sure to water the pots when they need it.

If your basement has a set of outside stairs with a storm cover, you

Watering trick

Ready to go

***Watering trick**. While bulbs are chilling, they need moist potting mix in which to make good roots. Enclosing a watered pot in a plastic bag (left), will keep the mix moist for a month or more. In the cold, the bulbs make roots, preparing themselves for spring and the return of warmth when they will make leaves and flowers. **Ready to go**. Removed from the pot, a group of grape hyacinths knits the potting mix together with plump white roots (above). When roots poke out the drainage hole and fill the pot, bulbs are ready to move into the light, where the pale shoots will quickly turn dark green.*

can also chill bulbs there. Late last fall, I set 48 pots of bulbs, closed inside plastic garbage bags, on the landing at the foot of my basement stairs, a spot that's about 4 ft. underground. For the next three months, the temperature there ranged from near-freezing to about 45°F—ideal for growing roots and chilling bulbs. Heat from the earth surrounded the containers; cold air poured down the stairs from the loose-fitting storm cover, but it was buffered by air in the 60's just 1 ft. away on the other side of the basement door.

Here come the flowers

When your bulbs have chilled for about three months, start checking their progress as indicted by root growth. Don't be misled into thinking they're ready to take out of the cold by a shoot poking up through the potting mix. To be sure about the bulbs, lift each pot and look at the bottom. If you see plump, white roots poking through the drainage holes, the bulbs are ready to come out of the cold.

The timing varies from one kind of bulb to another; some bulbs need just three months of chilling while others require four months, and some tulips may need five months (see the

forcing times on the chart on p. 91). You can always put pots that already have good roots back into the cold for a few more weeks.

When your bulbs are ready, bring them to a bright windowsill or sunroom. They need the light so their leaves and flower stems will grow short and sturdy—in weak light they'd produce tall and lanky flower stems that are likely to flop over.

Water the pots with care. Before leaves appear, you may have to water only every second or third day. Once

leaves appear, you may have to water every day. In both cases, wait until the surface of the potting mix is dry to the touch. If you want to keep the bulbs growing until spring so you can plant them in the garden as perennials, give them a weak solution of fertilizer from time to time.

Forcing does seem to shorten the bloom time of most bulbs. For example, indoors, grape hyacinths remain fragrant and presentable for about a week. Outdoors, they last two to three weeks. I think the difference has to do with temperature. Outdoors, in early spring, cool days and cold nights slow the onset of maturity. Indoor temperatures, however, stay close to 70°F both day and night, hastening the flowers' maturity and decline. To accommodate shortened bloom periods, force a lot of bulbs and bring only a few at a time to the windowsill. By staggering their bloom, you'll have plenty of bulbs either in flower or awaiting their turn in the cold. Your spring can begin as early as December and last until the outdoor trees leaf out. ∎

Mark Kane is the former editor of Fine Gardening *and is an ardent supporter of early springs.*

Index

The 22 articles in this book originally appeared in *Fine Gardening* magazine.
The date of first publication, issue number and page numbers for each article are given below.

If you enjoyed this book, you're going to love our magazine.

A year's subscription to *Fine Gardening* brings you the kind of hands-on information you found in this book, and much more. In issue after issue—six times a year—you'll find articles on nurturing specific plants, landscape design, fundamentals and building structures. Expert gardeners will share their knowledge and techniques with you. They will show you how to apply their knowledge in your own backyard. Filled with detailed illustrations and full-color photographs, *Fine Gardening* will inspire you to create and realize your dream garden!

To subscribe, just fill out one of the attached subscription cards or call us at 1-203-426-8171. And as always, your satisfaction is guaranteed, or we'll give you your money back.

Taunton
BOOKS & VIDEOS
for fellow enthusiasts

The Taunton Press 63 S. Main Street, P.O. Box 5506, Newtown, CT 06470-5506

Taunton
M A G A Z I N E S
for fellow enthusiasts

NO POSTAGE
NECESSARY
IF MAILED
IN THE
UNITED STATES

BUSINESS REPLY MAIL
FIRST CLASS MAIL   PERMIT NO.19   NEWTOWN CT

POSTAGE WILL BE PAID BY ADDRESSEE

FINE GARDENING®

63 SOUTH MAIN STREET
PO BOX 5506
NEWTOWN CT 06470-9955